Contents

"**I** love reading poetry with my students, but I just don't know how to teach them to read a poem and respond to it." Are you one of countless teachers who share this sentiment? If so, the simple, structured lessons of *Read and Understand Poetry* are just what you need!

- Easy-to-follow lessons guide you in introducing and reading poems chosen especially for students at your grade level.

- Quick and easy minilessons help you work with your students on the language arts skills that are unique to poetry.

- Individual follow-up activity pages help students consolidate what they have learned and extend their critical thinking and creativity.

What's on the Teacher Page?

The **teacher page** provides a simple, easy-to-follow lesson plan that includes these features:

The **Before You Read** section provides important background information for you to share with students prior to reading the poem. Guidelines for developing key concepts and suggestions for preteaching vocabulary are found here.

The **While You Read** section helps you choose the best way for students to experience each poem for the first time (such as listening to you read it aloud, reading it aloud chorally or individually, reading it silently, etc.).

The **After You Read** section guides you in presenting minilessons that focus on different types of poetry and on important elements of the language arts curriculum for poetry.

What's on the Poem Page?

Each **poem page** presents:

- the text of the poetry featured in the lesson

- a simple illustration to enhance comprehension

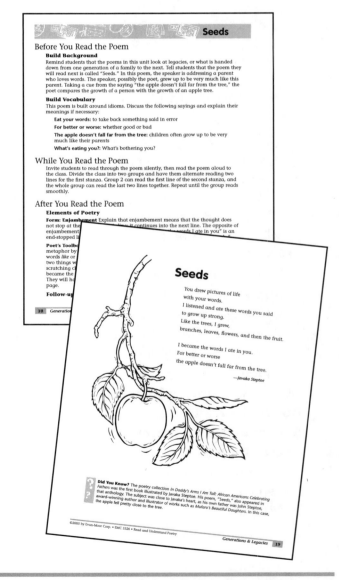

Read and Understand Poetry • EMC 3326 • ©2005 by Evan-Moor Corp.

snowflakes
slip from the sky
like soft white butterflies

...gs into a nut.

...ly...
under the moo...

Josiah

What's on the Follow-up Activity Pages?

As you guide students through the lessons outlined on the teacher page, they will have multiple opportunities to work as part of a group on developing an understanding of the form and content of each poem. The Follow-up Activities give students the opportunity to synthesize new information and practice language arts skills introduced during teacher-directed minilessons.

The first page of **Follow-up Activities** is designed to help students consolidate their comprehension of the poem by having them select the only correct response out of four possible choices for each of these multiple-choice items. Item content covers:

- literal comprehension
- sequence
- word meanings
- context clues and inferences
- main idea and details

In addition, the item format on this first activity page emulates the format students are likely to encounter on standardized language arts tests. After completing the activity pages in *Read and Understand Poetry*, students will be undaunted when a poem is presented as a reading passage on their next standardized test.

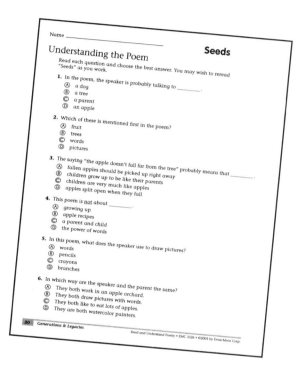

Name _____

Understanding the Poem   **Seeds**

Read each question and choose the best answer. You may wish to reread "Seeds" as you work.

1. In the poem, the speaker is probably talking to _____.
   Ⓐ a dog
   Ⓑ a tree
   Ⓒ a parent
   Ⓓ an apple

2. Which of these is mentioned first in the poem?
   Ⓐ fruit
   Ⓑ trees
   Ⓒ words
   Ⓓ pictures

3. The saying "the apple doesn't fall far from the tree" probably means that ____.
   Ⓐ fallen apples should be picked up right away
   Ⓑ children grow up to be like their parents
   Ⓒ children are very much like apples
   Ⓓ apples split open when they fall

4. This poem is _not_ about _____.
   Ⓐ growing up
   Ⓑ apple recipes
   Ⓒ a parent and child
   Ⓓ the power of words

5. In this poem, what does the speaker use to draw pictures?
   Ⓐ words
   Ⓑ pencils
   Ⓒ crayons
   Ⓓ branches

6. In which way are the speaker and the parent the same?
   Ⓐ They both work in an apple orchard.
   Ⓑ They both draw pictures with words.
   Ⓒ They both like to eat lots of apples.
   Ⓓ They are both watercolor painters.

30   *Generations & Legacies*   Read and Understand Poetry • EMC 3326 • ©2005 by Evan-Moor Corp.

Name _____   **Seeds**

Understanding the Poem

1. Remember that a simile compares two things by using the words *like* or *as*. Write a simile from "Seeds" below.

2. Remember that a metaphor compares two things without using the words *like* or *as*. Write the metaphor used in "Seeds" to describe the act of speaking.

3. Match each idiom in the left column with its meaning.

   The apple doesn't fall far from the tree.   Children grow into adults.
   What's eating you?   What's bothering you?
   He ate his words.   whether good or bad
   for better or worse   Children are like their parents.
   Mighty oaks from tiny acorns grow.   He admitted his mistake.

4. In the last stanza, before observing that "the apple doesn't fall far from the tree," the speaker says, "For better or worse." Why do you think that phrase is included?

5. When a thought does not stop at the end of a line but continues into the next line, it is called *enjambment*. When the thought begins and ends in the same line, the line has an *end stop*. Reread "Seeds," then write *enjambment* or *end stop* after each line below.

   a. You drew pictures of life   _____
   b. with your words.   _____
   c. I listened and ate these words you said _____
   d. to grow up strong.   _____
   e. Like the trees, I grew,   _____
   f. branches, leaves, flowers, and then the fruit. _____
   g. I became the words I ate in you. _____
   h. For better or worse   _____
   i. the apple doesn't fall far from the tree. _____

   ©2005 by Evan-Moor Corp. • EMC 3326 • Read and Understand Poetry   *Generations & Legacies*   21

The second page of **Follow-up Activities** may focus on any aspect of the language arts curriculum touched upon in the poem. Students may be invited to share their opinions as they respond to open-ended questions, to try their hand at using poetic techniques such as onomatopoeia or alliteration, or to write a poem of their own. Critical thinking and creativity are encouraged on this type of activity page.

snowflakes
slip from the sky
like soft white butterflies

What Are the Additional Student Resources?

A seven-page **Glossary of Poetry Terms** features kid-friendly definitions and pronunciation guidelines for terms ranging from *alliteration* to *simile*. Each glossary entry includes an example drawn from this anthology, further strengthening students' connection to poetry terminology.

An **About the Poets** feature presents brief, high-interest information on each of the poets included in this anthology. This helps build the additional context that allows students to deepen their understanding of the work of specific poets.

Designed for classroom display, the **Poetry Posters** present key elements and forms of poetry in a clear graphic format.

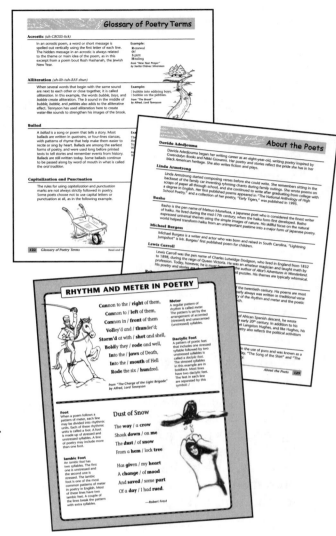

How to Use These Materials

To create a unique poetry anthology for your students, reproduce for each student:

- the cover page for the student *Read & Understand Poetry Anthology*

- the table of contents for each unit

- the poem and follow-up activity pages for each poem

- the Glossary of Poetry Terms and About the Poets pages

Place these pages together in a folder or three-ring binder to create individual poetry anthologies.

As students encounter new poems in their ongoing reading, they can use this resource to help them enjoy and deepen their knowledge of this timeless art form.

Generations & Legacies

Contents

Before You Read the Poem

Build Background

Tell students that the poems in this unit will look at generations in families and their legacies—what they hand down—to those who come after. Tell students that the poem they will read next is called "Artist to Artist." It expresses a writer's compassion for her gifted father, who was never able to realize his dreams of becoming a painter. Invite students to brainstorm different types of artists. Note that musicians, dancers, writers, sculptors, singers, and actors are also artists.

Build Vocabulary

Encourage students to give meanings for these idioms:

> **black and blue:** bruised
>
> **meat on their bones:** not skinny

While You Read the Poem

Invite students to read through the poem silently one or two times, then invite a volunteer to read it aloud to the class. Students may enjoy hearing the poem read aloud several times by different readers. Encourage all students who wish to try reading it aloud.

After You Read the Poem

Elements of Poetry

Poet's Toolbox: Multiple-Meaning Words Remind students that many words can have more than one meaning. Poets often choose words that mean more than one thing in order to bring richer meaning to their work. Ask students to find the color words that appear in the poem *(flesh-colored, black, blue);* discuss how these words relate to the meaning of the poem. Point out "black and blue" in the line "my father rode the bus feeling black and blue." Ask students to share any meanings these words might have. Could *black* refer to the father's identity as an African American? Might *blue* refer to a sad feeling, like the feelings expressed in the African American musical form called *the blues?* Might the father be feeling bruised or hurt? Encourage students to speculate about these ideas and to appreciate the multiple layers of interpretation introduced through the use of these words.

Poet's Toolbox: Repetition Review with students the meaning of repetition. You might say: *Writers often repeat words and phrases to create rhythm in a poem.* Encourage students to find words and phrases that are repeated in "Artist to Artist." Point out that sometimes most of a phrase is repeated, but a few words are changed. Ask what effect these small changes have on the sound and meaning of the poem.

Follow-up Activities

Students may work independently to complete the activities on pages 8 and 9.

Artist to Artist

I write books, now, because my father wanted
to be an artist when he grew up & he was good
at it, too. Drew people with meat on their bones
in flesh-colored tones from my 64-colors box
of crayons. But
every night—& sometimes even weekends & holidays—
he dressed in the blue uniform & black shoes
of many other fathers who also weren't doctors or lawyers,
teachers or preachers, & rode the 10:00 p.m. bus
to the downtown post office. Sorted mail by zip code—
60620, 60621, 60622. He sorted mail all night &
into the day because we had bills to pay. For 30 years
my father rode the bus feeling black and blue. He
never drew & his degrees in art and education sat
hardening on a shelf along with his oils
& acrylics. But

along with his gapped teeth, his bow legs & his first name
with an A at the end, he gave me the urge to create
characters with meat on their bones, in flesh-colored tones
written in words as vivid as a 64-colors box of crayons.
I write, he drew. Daddy, thank you!
& now that you're
retired...

...what do you want to be?

—*Davida Adedjouma*

Understanding the Poem

Read each question and choose the best answer. You may wish to reread "Artist to Artist" as you work.

1. What did the poet's father do for a living?
   - Ⓐ worked as a writer
   - Ⓑ worked as a musician
   - Ⓒ worked as a visual artist
   - Ⓓ worked for the post office

2. Which of these is mentioned first in the poem?
   - Ⓐ the father's job
   - Ⓑ the father's paints
   - Ⓒ the box of crayons
   - Ⓓ the poet's profession

3. "Acrylics" are probably _____.
   - Ⓐ false teeth
   - Ⓑ lost letters
   - Ⓒ paints for artists
   - Ⓓ academic degrees

4. This poem is mainly about _____.
   - Ⓐ writing
   - Ⓑ painting
   - Ⓒ thankfulness
   - Ⓓ the post office

5. What has the poet inherited from her father?
   - Ⓐ a talent for painting
   - Ⓑ the urge to create
   - Ⓒ money for college
   - Ⓓ a job at the post office

6. What was the poet's father's first name?
   - Ⓐ David
   - Ⓑ Steven
   - Ⓒ Michael
   - Ⓓ Jackson

Understanding the Poem

1. The poet and the speaker are the same in this poem. How do we know?

_____

_____

2. How does Davida feel about her father's years working in the post office? Explain your answer.

_____

_____

_____

3. Was Davida's father still living when she wrote this poem? Explain your answer.

_____

_____

_____

4. Find a word in the poem that rhymes with each of these words, and then add some more words to each rhyming family.

bones	grew	day	teachers
_____	_____	_____	_____
_____	_____	_____	_____
_____	_____	_____	_____
_____	_____	_____	_____

5. List some jobs that aren't "doctors or lawyers, teachers or preachers."

_____

_____

6. On the back of this paper, write a short poem about an adult you know who dreamed of doing something special.

Before You Read the Poem

Build Background

Remind students that the poems in this unit are about families across generations and their legacies. Tell students that the poem they are going to read is called "Her Daddy's Hands." In this poem, the narrator's mother tells about the strong, yet gentle hands of her hardworking father (the narrator's grandfather). Invite students to share information about members of their own families who work hard. The poem's story is set in Alabama. Explain that northern Alabama has red clay hills and that bricks are made from that clay. Have students find Alabama on a U.S. map.

While You Read the Poem

Invite students to read through the poem silently one or two times, then select a volunteer to read it aloud. Invite the class to join in on the lines "His hands, you see," and "those hands, you see." Lead half of the class in reading the first six lines, then lead the other half in reading the next six lines. Have the entire class read the last line together. Students may enjoy choosing partners to present the poem. Allow performers to practice for a few minutes before presenting their interpretations to the group.

After You Read the Poem

Elements of Poetry

Form: Free Verse Tell students that this poem is written as free verse. It does not use a pattern of repeated rhyme or rhythm, but it does use repeated sounds to create a musical quality and to emphasize meaning. Have students find words that have a long *o* sound as in *those*. Encourage them to look for other repeated vowel or consonant sounds, as well as for phrases that repeat or are slightly modified.

Poet's Toolbox: Narrative Voice Discuss with students the meaning of narrative voice. Three characters appear in "Her Daddy's Hands": the narrator, her mother, and her grandfather. Ask how many of those characters speak. Point out that the narrator is not necessarily the poet. The narrator in a poem is called the *speaker*. Explain that in this piece the poet has chosen to use colloquial, or natural speech, rather than formal speech. Ask the students how this choice of language contributes to the meaning of the poem.

Follow-up Activities

Students may work independently to complete the activities on pages 12 and 13.

Her Daddy's Hands

His hands, you see, Mama says
were hard and callused.
They worked all day making bricks
that made houses he'd show her
as he flew his noisy pick-up down the red
Alabama roads.
But on Sundays,
those hands, you see
felt soft,
and would hold my mama's and walk her to church.
Quietly.
Him in black, her in white
along those red Alabama roads.

—*Angela Johnson*

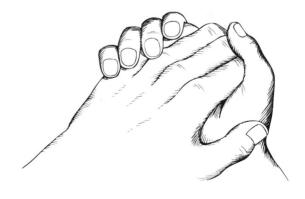

Understanding the Poem

Read each question and choose the best answer. You may wish to reread
"Her Daddy's Hands" as you work.

1. In the poem, what was Daddy's job?

Ⓐ a builder

Ⓑ a preacher

Ⓒ a truck driver

Ⓓ a brick maker

2. Which of these is mentioned first in the poem?

Ⓐ Mama's daddy works all day.

Ⓑ Mama's daddy shows her houses.

Ⓒ Mama walks to church with her daddy.

Ⓓ Mama rides with her daddy in the pick-up.

3. The word *callused* probably means _____.

Ⓐ softened

Ⓑ bleached

Ⓒ weakened

Ⓓ toughened

4. This poem is <u>not</u> about _____.

Ⓐ a brick maker

Ⓑ a loving daughter

Ⓒ city life in Alabama

Ⓓ hearing family stories

5. How does the speaker's mother probably feel about her father?

Ⓐ fears him

Ⓑ loves him

Ⓒ resents him

Ⓓ feels confused

6. Mama's father worked hard because he _____.

Ⓐ wanted to be rich

Ⓑ wanted to be famous

Ⓒ loved his work more than anything else

Ⓓ loved his family and wanted to care for them

Understanding the Poem

1. Antonyms are words that have opposite meanings. "Her Daddy's Hands" uses antonyms to show two sides of the father's character. List an antonym for each of these words from the poem. Use a dictionary or thesaurus if you need to.

   noisy   **calloused**   **quietly**   **soft**

   _____   _____   _____   _____

2. "Her Daddy's Hands" is written as free verse, so it does not have a rhyme pattern, but it does use repetition to create "word music." Find two phrases that are repeated, with slight variations, in the poem. Write them below.

   _____

   _____

3. *Synecdoche* is the use of a part of something to represent the whole thing. In "Her Daddy's Hands," the words *calloused hands* stand for the speaker's hardworking grandfather. Each sentence on the left uses synecdoche. Draw a line to the sentence on the right that the words stand for.

   It was delivered to our door.   I'll help you.

   She has her nose in our business.   They brought it to our house.

   He has new wheels.   She gets involved in our business.

   I'll give you a hand.   He has a new car.

   Work with a partner to think of another example of synecdoche. Write your example here.

   _____

4. How is Mama's father different on Sundays than on other days of the week?

   _____

   _____

   _____

Before You Read the Poem

Build Background

Remind students that the poems in this unit are about generations and the legacies of families. Tell students that the poem they will read next is called "Grandmother Had One Good Coat." It takes place in a city where there are homeless people living under the elevated commuter train station. Encourage students to share their thoughts about homelessness. You may wish to wrap up the discussion by noting that homelessness often brings out a feeling of compassion, or concerned sympathy, in others.

Build Vocabulary

Encourage students to give meanings for these words and phrase. Introduce any that are unfamiliar.

depressed: sad

elevated: raised; lifted up above

hesitation: pause

passersby: people walking by

patent leather: a type of shiny leather, often used for fancy shoes

scowl: <u>frown</u>

taunting: teasing; baiting; insulting

While You Read the Poem

Invite students to read through the poem silently, then invite a different volunteer to read each stanza aloud. Form two groups of students. Lead each group in reading alternate stanzas of the poem.

After You Read the Poem

Elements of Poetry

Form: Narrative Verse Explain that a poem that tells a story is called a narrative poem. Encourage students to retell the story in their own words. Prompt students to identify the setting, characters, story problem, and solution. Discuss whether the ending was expected or unexpected.

Poet's Toolbox: Creative Format Point out that, except for the title and the word *I*, there are no capital letters or punctuation marks in "My Grandmother Had One Good Coat." Help students notice how the title in this poem is unusual because it also serves as the first line of the poem. Point out the phrase "without hesitation" in the last stanza. Ask students to find two different ways to read the first three lines of that stanza. Discuss how the lack of punctuation allows this phrase to be read two different ways. At the same time, it helps show how both the speaker and the grandmother have no hesitation in showing compassion for the needy.

Follow-up Activities

Students may work independently to complete the activities on pages 16 and 17.

My Grandmother Had One Good Coat

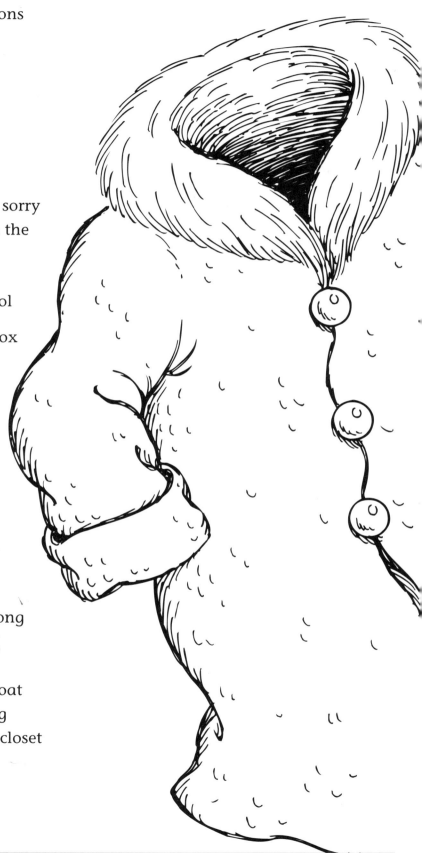

a black wool one with black buttons
shiny as patent leather shoes
and a smooth furry collar
just as black

she wore this only
to the doctor or to church

one late afternoon
I came home from school feeling sorry
for an old woman living beneath the
elevated train below the station
who sat taunting passersby
on their way to work and to school

she sat coatless on a cardboard box
hiding her pain behind
curses and scowls

she could have been
my own grandmother

and the thought of my own
grandmother homeless
in the cold with no place
to pray and be warm
made me sad and depressed

when she asked me what was wrong
and I told her, without hesitation,
she went into her closet
and handed me her black dress coat
and said here put it in a shopping
bag you'll find one in the broom closet
I don't use it that much anyway

—*Tony Medina*

Understanding the Poem

Read each question and choose the best answer. You may wish to reread
"My Grandmother Had One Good Coat" as you work.

1. Where does this poem take place?
   - Ⓐ in the city
   - Ⓑ at school
   - Ⓒ on a farm
   - Ⓓ on a train

2. Which of these is mentioned first in the poem?
   - Ⓐ the broom closet
   - Ⓑ the cardboard box
   - Ⓒ the black wool coat
   - Ⓓ the homeless woman

3. An elevated train probably travels _____.
   - Ⓐ as fast as an elevator
   - Ⓑ on tracks under the city
   - Ⓒ up and down tall buildings
   - Ⓓ on tracks that go above city streets

4. This poem is <u>not</u> about _____.
   - Ⓐ a homeless woman
   - Ⓑ riding commuter trains
   - Ⓒ a compassionate child
   - Ⓓ a generous grandmother

5. Which word best describes the speaker's grandmother?
   - Ⓐ hungry
   - Ⓑ wealthy
   - Ⓒ generous
   - Ⓓ depressed

6. Where did the speaker probably learn to care about the less fortunate?
   - Ⓐ at school
   - Ⓑ from television
   - Ⓒ from his grandmother
   - Ⓓ from movies and books

Understanding the Poem

1. Words with the same meanings are called *synonyms*. Connect each word in the first column with its synonym in the second column.

scowl	pause
depressed	mock
elevate	frown
hesitate	raise
taunt	sad

2. According to the speaker, how was the homeless woman behaving, and why was she acting that way?

_____

_____

3. Do the grandmother and the speaker live together? Give reasons to support your answer.

_____

_____

4. Does the missing capitalization and punctuation help or hurt the poem? Give reasons for your answer.

_____

_____

5. How are the grandmother and the speaker the same?

_____

_____

6. How are the grandmother and the homeless woman the same?

_____

_____

7. How does the grandmother teach the speaker about kindness?

_____

_____

Before You Read the Poem

Build Background

Remind students that the poems in this unit look at legacies, or what is handed down from one generation of a family to the next. Tell students that the poem they will read next is called "Seeds." In this poem, the speaker is addressing a parent who loves words. The speaker, possibly the poet, grew up to be very much like this parent. Taking a cue from the saying "the apple doesn't fall far from the tree," the poet compares the growth of a person with the growth of an apple tree.

Build Vocabulary

This poem is built around idioms. Discuss the following sayings and explain their meanings if necessary:

Eat your words: to take back something said in error

For better or worse: whether good or bad

The apple doesn't fall far from the tree: children often grow up to be very much like their parents

What's eating you?: What's bothering you?

While You Read the Poem

Invite students to read through the poem silently, then read the poem aloud to the class. Divide the class into two groups and have them alternate reading two lines for the first stanza. Group 2 can read the first line of the second stanza, and the whole group can read the last two lines together. Repeat until the group reads smoothly.

After You Read the Poem

Elements of Poetry

Form: Enjambement Explain that enjambement means that the thought does not stop at the end of a poetic line; it continues into the next line. The opposite of enjambement is a line with an end stop. "I became the words I ate in you" is an end-stopped line. Invite students to find examples of enjambement in "Seeds."

Poet's Toolbox: Metaphor and Simile Explain the difference between simile and metaphor by sharing these examples: A simile compares two things by using the words *like* or *as*. Example: "The branch scratched *like* a claw." A metaphor compares two things without using the words *like* or *as*. Example: "The branch was a scratching claw." Work with students to find examples of the use of metaphor ("I became the words I ate in you") and simile ("Like the trees, I grew") in "Seeds." They will have the opportunity to practice this independently on the second activity page.

Follow-up Activities

Students may work independently to complete the activities on pages 20 and 21.

Seeds

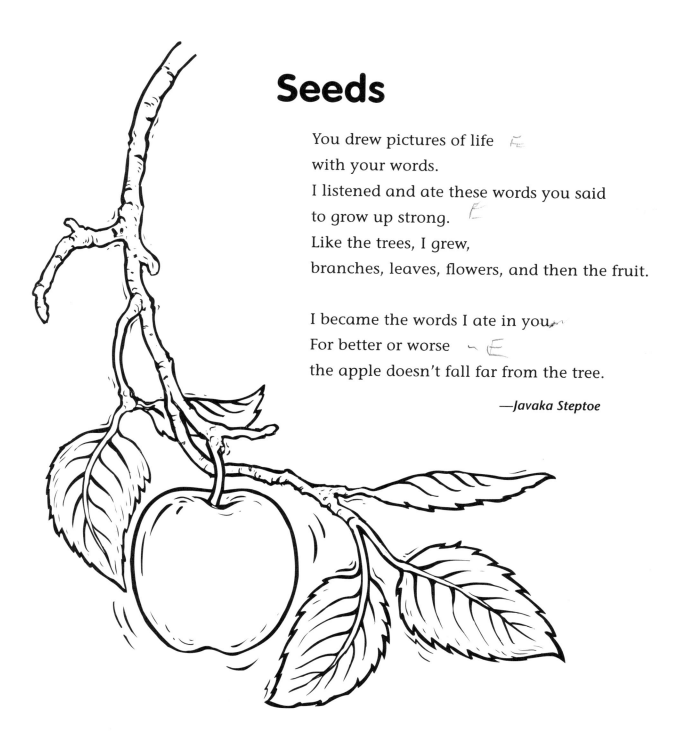

You drew pictures of life
with your words.
I listened and ate these words you said
to grow up strong.
Like the trees, I grew,
branches, leaves, flowers, and then the fruit.

I became the words I ate in you.
For better or worse
the apple doesn't fall far from the tree.

—*Javaka Steptoe*

Did You Know? The poetry collection *In Daddy's Arms I Am Tall: African Americans Celebrating Fathers* was the first book illustrated by Javaka Steptoe. His poem, "Seeds," also appeared in that anthology. The subject was close to Javaka's heart, as his own father was John Steptoe, award-winning author and illustrator of works such as *Mufaro's Beautiful Daughters*. In this case, the apple fell pretty close to the tree.

Seeds

Understanding the Poem

Read each question and choose the best answer. You may wish to reread "Seeds" as you work.

1. In the poem, the speaker is probably talking to _____ .
   - Ⓐ a dog
   - Ⓑ a tree
   - Ⓒ a parent
   - Ⓓ an apple

2. Which of these is mentioned first in the poem?
   - Ⓐ fruit
   - Ⓑ trees
   - Ⓒ words
   - Ⓓ pictures

3. The saying "the apple doesn't fall far from the tree" probably means that _____ .
   - Ⓐ fallen apples should be picked up right away
   - Ⓑ children grow up to be like their parents
   - Ⓒ children are very much like apples
   - Ⓓ apples split open when they fall

4. This poem is <u>not</u> about _____ .
   - Ⓐ growing up
   - Ⓑ apple recipes
   - Ⓒ a parent and child
   - Ⓓ the power of words

5. In this poem, what does the speaker use to draw pictures?
   - Ⓐ words
   - Ⓑ pencils
   - Ⓒ crayons
   - Ⓓ branches

6. In which way are the speaker and the parent the same?
   - Ⓐ They both work in an apple orchard.
   - Ⓑ They both draw pictures with words.
   - Ⓒ They both like to eat lots of apples.
   - Ⓓ They are both watercolor painters.

Seeds

Understanding the Poem

1. Remember that a simile compares two things by using the words *like* or *as*. Write a simile from "Seeds" below.

_____

2. Remember that a metaphor compares two things without using the words *like* or *as*. Write the metaphor used in "Seeds" to describe the act of speaking.

_____

3. Match each idiom in the left column with its meaning.

The apple doesn't fall far from the tree.	Children grow into adults.
What's eating you?	What's bothering you?
He ate his words.	whether good or bad
for better or worse	Children are like their parents.
Mighty oaks from tiny acorns grow.	He admitted his mistake.

4. In the last stanza, before observing that "the apple doesn't fall far from the tree," the speaker says, "For better or worse." Why do you think that phrase is included?

_____

_____

5. When a thought does not stop at the end of a line but continues into the next line, it is called *enjambement*. When the thought begins and ends in the same line, the line has an *end stop*. Reread "Seeds," then write *enjambement* or *end stop* after each line below.

a. You drew pictures of life _____

b. with your words. _____

c. I listened and ate these words you said _____

d. to grow up strong. _____

e. Like the trees, I grew, _____

f. branches, leaves, flowers, and then the fruit. _____

g. I became the words I ate in you. _____

h. For better or worse _____

i. the apple doesn't fall far from the tree. _____

Before You Read the Poem

Build Background

Remind students that in this unit, poets look at connections between generations in families. Tell students that the poem they will read next is called "The Farmer." It takes place in Georgia at a time when fields were still tilled with a plow and mule. With the words *forged* and *iron*, the poet builds a metaphor that compares an African American farmer's hardships to the tempering, or hardening, of steel. Soil, or clay, is important in both farming and the making of steel. Heat is also a factor in both.

Build Vocabulary

Encourage students to give meanings for these words. Explain any that are unfamiliar.

forged: shaped by the heat of a fire in a special stove used to work with metal

plot: piece of land

stern: strict; serious

While You Read the Poem

Invite students to read through the poem silently one or two times, then invite a volunteer to read it aloud to the class. Accentuate the list structure of the poem by having a different student read each line. Have the entire group read the last three lines together.

After You Read the Poem

Elements of Poetry

Form: Rhyming Verse Tell students that this poem has meter, or a definite rhythm pattern, and rhyme. Invite students to find the rhyming words. Have them find two other words that are "near rhymes" (*sweat* and *hat*). Challenge them to point out how the rhyme scheme changes in the last three lines of the poem. Point out that the poem also changes from a list to a metaphor in the last three lines, as the poet comments on the farmer's strength by noting how his backbone, representing his personal strength, has been strengthened by his African heritage and his connection to the land he works.

Poet's Toolbox: Metaphor Explain that steel is stronger than iron, but tempered steel is even harder than steel. Steel is tempered when a blacksmith reheats it in a forge and hammers on it. Then it is carefully cooled. A coating of clay is used in the cooling process. Ask students to comment on how the life of the farmer is compared with the tempering, or strengthening, of steel.

Follow-up Activities

Students may work independently to complete the activities on pages 24 and 25.

The Farmer

A plot of weeds,
an old grey mule.
Hot sun and sweat
on a bright Southern day.
Strong, stern papa
under a straw hat,
plowing and planting
his whole life away.
His backbone is forged
of African iron
and red Georgia clay.

—*Carole Boston Weatherford*

Understanding the Poem

Read each question and choose the best answer. You may wish to reread "The Farmer" as you work.

1. Where does this poem take place?

- Ⓐ California
- Ⓑ Georgia
- Ⓒ Maine
- Ⓓ Ohio

2. Which of these is mentioned first in the poem?

- Ⓐ the farm
- Ⓑ the heat
- Ⓒ the work
- Ⓓ the mule

3. A *plot* is probably _____.

- Ⓐ a farmhouse
- Ⓑ a kind of plow
- Ⓒ a piece of land
- Ⓓ a farm machine

4. This poem is not about _____.

- Ⓐ cotton
- Ⓑ strength
- Ⓒ a farmer
- Ⓓ hard work

5. Which of these words best describes the farmer in the poem?

- Ⓐ rich
- Ⓑ lazy
- Ⓒ weary
- Ⓓ strong

6. What does the farmer do in his spare time?

- Ⓐ He paints pictures.
- Ⓑ He makes straw hats.
- Ⓒ He has no spare time.
- Ⓓ He can't decide what to do.

Understanding the Poem

1. Some words have more than one meaning. Write the word in the poem that fits each pair of meanings below.

<table>
<tr><td>a storyline
a piece of land</td><td>to smooth out wrinkles
a type of metal</td><td>the back end of a ship
serious</td></tr>
<tr><td>_____</td><td>_____</td><td>_____</td></tr>
</table>

2. The first four lines of "The Farmer" set the scene. In your own words, tell where the farmer is, what the weather is like, and who is with him.

_____

_____

3. The first seven lines of "The Farmer" create a picture of the scene in the poem by listing various elements. Read the following list and cross out any items that are not "shown" in the poem.

a. a father wearing a straw hat

b. a man plowing with a mule

c. an old rusty tractor

d. rustling rows of cornstalks

e. a hot sun blazing in the sky

f. a field that needs plowing

g. a broken-down shack

h. giraffes, rhinos, and lions

i. an African American farmer

j. a man serious about his work

4. In the last three lines of the poem, the narrator says, "His backbone is forged of African iron and red Georgia clay." *Backbone* is a word often used to describe courage and strength. What is the narrator saying about the farmer's character?

_____

_____

_____

Seasons of Life

Contents

Before You Read the Poem

Build Background

Explain to students that the poems in this unit are about seasons—both those that we experience throughout the cycle of the year as well as those that mark the cycle of a lifetime. Tell them that the poem they will read next is called "No!" and is about the month of November. It is by Thomas Hood, a British poet and humorist who lived in the 1800s. Hood's serious poems such as "Song of the Shirt" are still widely read, but his funny verses were more famous in his own time. Invite students to share what their associations for the month of November are, and what they like and dislike about that month.

Build Vocabulary

Language is always changing. New words are invented and old words disappear. Word meanings shift and evolve. This poem was written more than a hundred and fifty years ago. Invite students to give today's definitions for the following words. When necessary, explain the older meanings (noted below).

ease: comfort; rest

feel: feeling

healthful: healthy

member: part of the body, such as an arm or leg

shine: light or good weather; sunshine

While You Read the Poem

Invite students to read through the poem silently one or two times, then have a volunteer read it aloud to the class. Next, have a group of students read the poem aloud, each one taking a different "No" phrase such as "No sun." Have the whole class join in for the last line.

After You Read the Poem

Elements of Poetry

Poet's Toolbox: Repetition Help students focus on the repetition of the word *no* in the poem. It is used to begin each line except the last. In addition, all except one of those lines repeats the word *no* once, twice, or three more times. Discuss how this repeated use of the word *no* helps create a dreary, negative image of November. The occurrence of *no* in the first syllable of *November* in the last line adds an element of surprise. After 44 repetitions of the word *no*, readers expect that this line, too, will begin with *no*, so it is a surprise to hear the single final word: *November*.

Follow-up Activities

Students may work independently to complete the activities on pages 29 and 30.

No!

1 No sun—no moon!
No morn—no noon!
No dawn—no dusk—no proper time of day—
No sky—no earthly view—
5 No distance looking blue—
No road—no street—no "t'other side this way"—
No end to any Row—
No indications where the Crescents go—
No top to any steeple—
10 No recognitions of familiar people—
No courtesies for showing 'em—
No knowing 'em!
No traveling at all—no locomotion—
No inkling of the way—no notion—
15 "No go" by land or ocean—
No mail—no post—
No news from any foreign coast—
No Park, no Ring, no afternoon gentility—
No company—no nobility—
20 No warmth, no cheerfulness, no healthful ease,
No comfortable feel in any member—
No shade, no shine, no butterflies, no bees,
No fruits, no flowers, no leaves, no birds—
November!

—*Thomas Hood*

No!

Understanding the Poem

Read each question and choose the best answer. You may wish to reread "No!" as you work.

1. Which of these is <u>not</u> mentioned in the poem?
- Ⓐ ease
- Ⓑ grass
- Ⓒ moon
- Ⓓ warmth

2. Which of these is mentioned first in the poem?
- Ⓐ noon
- Ⓑ leaves
- Ⓒ flowers
- Ⓓ comfort

3. The word *morn* probably means _____.
- Ⓐ storm
- Ⓑ sadness
- Ⓒ morning
- Ⓓ warning

4. This poem is mainly about _____.
- Ⓐ October
- Ⓑ Monday
- Ⓒ Saturday
- Ⓓ November

5. Which of these words would best describe the month of November?
- Ⓐ sunny
- Ⓑ gloomy
- Ⓒ cheerful
- Ⓓ healthful

6. How does the speaker feel about November?
- Ⓐ He thinks it's terrible.
- Ⓑ He thinks it's all right.
- Ⓒ It's his favorite month.
- Ⓓ He wants it to last all year.

Understanding the Poem

1. In the line 22, what would be another way to say "no shade, no shine"?

   _____

2. The word *healthful* is formed by adding the suffix *-ful* to the word *health*. The new word means "full of health." Write a definition for each of these words that also end with the suffix *-ful.*

   cheerful _____   **wasteful** _____

   careful _____   **artful** _____

   thoughtful _____   **fearful** _____

3. The word *cheerfulness* has two suffixes: *-ful* and *-ness*. With this second suffix, the new word means "the state of being full of cheer," or "the state of being cheerful." Write a definition for these words that each have two suffixes.

   wastefulness _____

   thoughtfulness _____

4. Thomas Hood uses rhyming words to help shape his poem. For each of these words, find a rhyming word from the poem.

   moon _____   **ease** _____

   steeple _____   **member** _____

5. Another way that poets add special sounds to their work is through the use of *alliteration*. An alliteration is created when two or more words that start with the same sound appear close together in the poem. Find the word that appears near each of the following words to create alliteration.

   moon _____   **butterflies** _____

   dawn _____   **fruits** _____

   shade _____

Before You Read the Poem

Build Background

Remind students that some of the poems in this unit look at the cycle of life. Tell them that the poem they will read next is an excerpt from a collection of poems called *Proverbs and Songs*. It was written by the Spanish poet Antonio Machado (1875–1939). It is about the human journey through life. It says that there is no right way to live. Each person invents his or her own life by living it. Prompt students to share their ideas about how life is like a journey. Ask: *Is there a map that tells us where to go? Can we see where we've already been? Do we know where we will end up?*

Build Vocabulary

Have students share the meaning of these words. Teach any that are unfamiliar.

blazing: making a path where there was none

gaze: look

lot: fate; role in life

pathways: routes

wake: trail left in the water by a boat or other moving object

wayfarer: traveler; wanderer

While You Read the Poem

Invite students to read through the poem silently one or two times. Have a different volunteer read each stanza. Then divide the class in half. Have the groups read alternating stanzas. Have students divide into small groups and let them decide how to present the poem. Allow time for rehearsal. Encourage students to share what they liked best about each presentation.

After You Read the Poem

Elements of Poetry

Form: Translation If you have fluent or native Spanish-speakers in your class, invite them to read Machado's original poem in Spanish. Point out that in creating a translation, translators try to capture the tone, feeling, and meaning of the original poem. Often, patterns of rhyme and rhythm from the original poem cannot be matched in the translation. That is the case with this translation of Machado's poem.

Poet's Toolbox: Repetition Invite students to find the words and phrases that are repeated in the poem. Notice how these words convey the central ideas of the poem: moving onward, making pathways, and wayfarers. Point out how the last line of the second stanza and the first line of the third stanza repeat the same words, but in a different order. How does this add interest to the poem? Students may compare these lines to the Spanish original and note that the translator faithfully echoed the original poem with this construction.

Follow-up Activities

Students may work independently to complete the activities on pages 33 and 34.

Wayfarer, There Is No Path

All things move on and all things stay,
but it is our lot to move on,
to move on blazing pathways,
pathways upon the sea.

Wayfarer, your footprints are
the pathway and nothing else;
wayfarer, there is no path,
the path is made as you walk.

As you walk the path is made
and when you gaze behind
you see the path where
you'll never walk again.

Wayfarer, there is no path,
just the wake upon the sea . . .

—Antonio Machado
from *Proverbs and Songs*
Translation by
Sarita Chávez Silverman

Caminante, no hay camino

Todo pasa y todo queda,
pero lo nuestro es pasar,
pasar haciendo caminos,
caminos sobre el mar.

Caminante, son tus huellas
el camino y nada más;
caminante, no hay camino,
se hace camino al andar.

Al andar se hace camino
y al volver la vista atrás
se ve la senda que nunca
se ha de volver a pisar.

Caminante no hay camino
sino estelas en la mar . . .

de "Proverbios y cantares"
por Antonio Machado

Understanding the Poem

Read each question and choose the best answer. You may wish to reread "Wayfarer, There Is No Path" as you work.

1. Which of these is <u>not</u> mentioned in the poem?
   - Ⓐ footprints
   - Ⓑ pathways
   - Ⓒ wayfarers
   - Ⓓ campfires

2. Which of these is mentioned first in the poem?
   - Ⓐ the wake on the water
   - Ⓑ a pathway of footprints
   - Ⓒ pathways blazed on the sea
   - Ⓓ a path you'll never walk again

3. The word *gaze* probably means _____.
   - Ⓐ to look
   - Ⓑ to think
   - Ⓒ to forget
   - Ⓓ to guess

4. This poem is <u>not</u> about _____.
   - Ⓐ a blazing fire
   - Ⓑ life as a journey
   - Ⓒ always moving on
   - Ⓓ making your own way

5. Which of these best describes the speaker's view of life?
   - Ⓐ You can't escape the past.
   - Ⓑ You cannot change your fate.
   - Ⓒ Your life is guided by the choices you make.
   - Ⓓ The actions of others keep you from success.

6. The phrase "there is no path" means that _____.
   - Ⓐ the speaker is lost in the woods
   - Ⓑ the path is covered with rocks and weeds
   - Ⓒ waves can wash away a path in the sand
   - Ⓓ each person must find his or her own way

Name _____

Understanding the Poem

1. The poet says, "All things move on and all things stay." Read the following sentences. Circle those that are examples of this idea. Cross out those that are not.

   a. Children grow up and become adults, but there are always children in the world.

   b. Mountain streams flow down to the sea, but the streams never dry up.

   c. You write a letter and send it off in the mail, and you never see it again.

   d. Students graduate, but new students come to the school.

   e. You take a trip, but you leave most of your things at home.

2. In the poem, the speaker talks about "blazing pathways upon the sea." Is this possible? Explain what this image means.

   _____

   _____

3. The suffix -er can turn a verb into a noun. Read the example below. Then complete the rest of the chart.

Word	Word + the suffix -er
Verb: wander **Meaning:** to walk around without heading for a specific destination	Noun: _wanderer_ Meaning: _a person who wanders_
Verb: teach **Meaning:** to provide instruction	Noun: _____ Meaning: _____
Verb: believe **Meaning:** to be convinced of something	Noun: _____ Meaning: _____
Verb: listen **Meaning:** to pay attention to words or sounds	Noun: _____ Meaning: _____
Verb: travel **Meaning:** to journey, or take a trip	Noun: _____ Meaning: _____
Verb: pretend **Meaning:** to act or make believe	Noun: _____ Meaning: _____

Before You Read the Poem

Build Background

Remind students that the poems in this unit are about seasons of the year and "seasons" of life. Tell students that the poem they will read next is called "Youth, I Do Adore Thee!" It is from a collection called *The Passionate Pilgrim.* Although the book was published under the name William Shakespeare, scholars think that most of the poems, including this one, may have been written by other writers from the same period.

Build Vocabulary

Some words in this poem have changed their meaning since Shakespeare's time, and other words have fallen out of use. Help students understand any of these words that are unfamiliar:

abhor: hate   **crabbed:** complaining; grouchy   **lame:** crippled; stiff

adore: love   **defy:** refuse to accept; challenge   **methinks:** I think

bold: brave; adventurous   **hie:** hurry; make haste   **nimble:** quick and light

While You Read the Poem

Invite students to listen as you read the poem aloud for them. (Note that the accent on *crabbèd* indicates that it should be read as a two-syllable word.) Read the poem a second time, this time asking students to follow along in their texts. Then have partners work together, one taking the lines relating to Youth, the other taking those relating to Age. After partners practice, invite volunteers to present readings for the class.

After You Read the Poem

Elements of Poetry

Form: Lyric Tell students that this poem is a rhymed lyric. Explain that lyric poetry focuses on sharing feelings and impressions. This poem also has a strong rhythm, or meter, and includes rhyming words. Ask students to circle words that rhyme. They will have more practice with these words on the second activity page.

Poet's Toolbox: Similes and Metaphors Remind students that a simile compares two things using the words *as* or *like,* as in this example: "The river wound through the valley *like* a blue ribbon." A metaphor compares two things, but does not include the words *as* or *like,* as in this example: "The river is a blue ribbon winding through the valley." Work with students to find examples of similes and metaphors in "Youth, I Do Adore Thee!" They will have additional practice with this on the second activity page.

Follow-up Activities

Students may work independently to complete the activities on pages 37 and 38.

Youth, I Do Adore Thee!

Crabbèd age and youth
Cannot live together:
Youth is full of pleasance,
Age is full of care;
Youth like summer morn,
Age like winter weather;
Youth like summer brave,
Age like winter bare.
Youth is full of sport,
Age's breath is short.

Youth is nimble, Age is lame,
Youth is hot and bold,
Age is weak and cold.
Youth is wild, and Age is tame.
   Age, I do abhor thee;
   Youth, I do adore thee.
     O my love, my love is young.
   Age, I do defy thee.
     O sweet shepherd, hie thee, *hie thee,*
For methinks thou stay'st too long.

—*William Shakespeare*
from *The Passionate Pilgrim*, **Part 12**

Understanding the Poem

Read each question and choose the best answer. You may wish to reread "Youth, I Do Adore Thee!" as you work.

1. Which of these is <u>not</u> mentioned in the poem?
   - Ⓐ shortness of breath
   - Ⓑ quickness
   - Ⓒ bad teeth
   - Ⓓ wildness

2. Which of these is mentioned first in the poem?
   - Ⓐ sport
   - Ⓑ winter weather
   - Ⓒ a summer morn
   - Ⓓ a sweet shepherd

3. The word *pleasance* probably means _____.
   - Ⓐ dancing
   - Ⓑ peasants
   - Ⓒ great sadness
   - Ⓓ pleasant things

4. This poem is mainly about _____.
   - Ⓐ heat and cold
   - Ⓑ youth and old age
   - Ⓒ summer and winter
   - Ⓓ strength and weakness

5. According to the speaker, which of these is true?
   - Ⓐ Age is best.
   - Ⓑ Youth is best.
   - Ⓒ Both are equally bad.
   - Ⓓ Both are equally good.

6. How does love make the speaker feel?
   - Ⓐ wild
   - Ⓑ weak
   - Ⓒ nimble
   - Ⓓ younger

Understanding the Poem

1. Antonyms are words that have opposite meanings. In this poem, the poet uses antonyms to point out the contrasts between youth and old age. Write the number that corresponds to an antonym for each word.

a. _5_ winter   **e.** _2_ wild   **1.** defy   **5.** summer

b. _3_ nimble   **f.** _7_ abhor   **2.** tame   **6.** cold

c. _6_ hot   **g.** _4_ age   **3.** sluggish **7.** adore

d. _8_ timid   **h.** _1_ obey   **4.** youth   **8.** bold

2. "Youth, I Do Adore Thee!" has many rhyming words. Write a rhyming word from the poem on each line, and then add another rhyming word of your own.

tame	bold	care	sport
lame	cold	bare	short
shame	bold	share	fort

3. A simile uses the words *like* or *as* to compare two things:

The river wound through the valley like a blue ribbon.

A metaphor compares two things, but does **not** include the words *as* or *like*:

The river is a blue ribbon winding through the valley.

Read each sentence and decide if it is a simile or a metaphor. Write **M** or **S** to show what you decide.

_M_ Youth is nimble.   _S_ Age <u>like</u> winter bare.

_S_ Age <u>like</u> winter weather.   _M_ Youth <u>is</u> wild.

_S_ Youth <u>like</u> summer brave.   _M_ Age <u>is</u> weak and cold.

4. Write a word from the poem that means the same thing as each of these words:

grouchy	crabbed
I think	methinks
you	thou
do stay	stay
morning	morn

Before You Read the Poem

Build Background

Remind students that this unit includes poems about the seasons of the year. Tell students that the poem they will read next is called "New Year Prayer." It is about Rosh Hashanah, the Jewish New Year. Rosh Hashanah is considered "the birthday of creation" and begins with the blast of the *shofar*, or ram's horn. If any students celebrate Rosh Hashanah, invite them to share their traditions. These might include eating special foods, such as apples dipped in honey to ensure a sweet year and bread shaped in a spiral as a reminder that the cycle of the year goes 'round and 'round, year after year.

Build Vocabulary

Encourage students to give meanings for these words. Provide definitions for any that they cannot articulate.

harmony: two or more elements fitting together in a pleasing or peaceful way

humanity: all human beings; the quality of being human; compassion

renewal: the act of making something new or fresh again

spirit: life force; essence

While You Read the Poem

Invite students to read through the poem silently. Choose a different student to read each line aloud. Explain that in music, a *rest* is a planned piece of silence. In many poems, commas and periods serve as rests, but in some poems, such as this one, there is no punctuation. Ask students where pauses could be included. Have volunteers read the poem with pauses in different places.

After You Read the Poem

Elements of Poetry

Form: Acrostic Explain that some poems are written to include extra meanings that cannot be heard when the poem is read aloud because they appear only in print. In an acrostic poem, a word or short message is spelled out by the first letter of each line. This message in an acrostic is always related to the theme of the poem. Invite students to discover what is spelled by the first letter of each line in "New Year Prayer."

Poet's Toolbox: Phraseology A phrase is a cluster of related words. Sometimes, a poet conveys a great deal of meaning through a simple phrase, even though the phrase does not form a complete sentence. In this poem, the poet has strung together a list of values and concepts that are all related to the spirit of Rosh Hashanah. Invite students to experiment with different ways of grouping the words into phrases.

Follow-up Activities

Students may work independently to complete the activities on pages 41 and 42.

New Year Prayer

Renewal
Of
Spirit
Healing
Heart
And
Soul
Harmony
Among
Nations
And
Humanity

—Sarita Chávez Silverman

Did You Know? Rosh Hashanah, the Jewish New Year, always begins on the first day of the Jewish month of Tishrei. In 2001, this date corresponded to Tuesday, September 18 on the Gregorian calendar (the calendar used in the United States and much of the world). This date was exactly one week after the events of September 11, 2001. This poem expresses the poet's hopes for healing and forgiveness following the tragic events of that day.

Read and Understand Poetry • EMC 3326 • ©2005 by Evan-Moor Corp.

Name _____

Understanding the Poem

Read each question and choose the best answer. You may wish to reread "New Year Prayer" as you work.

1. Which of these is <u>not</u> mentioned in the poem?
- Ⓐ harmony among nations
- Ⓑ hopes and fears
- Ⓒ renewal of spirit
- Ⓓ heart and soul

2. Which of these is mentioned last in the poem?
- Ⓐ humanity
- Ⓑ renewal
- Ⓒ healing
- Ⓓ heart

3. The word *soul* in the poem probably means _____.
- Ⓐ a part of a shoe
- Ⓑ a type of food
- Ⓒ a type of music
- Ⓓ a person's spirit

4. This poem is <u>not</u> about _____.
- Ⓐ a fresh start
- Ⓑ building a temple
- Ⓒ the Jewish New Year
- Ⓓ a prayer for peace and harmony

5. Which of these kinds of thoughts are best to keep in mind on Rosh Hashanah?
- Ⓐ selfish and greedy
- Ⓑ fearful and nervous
- Ⓒ hopeful and positive
- Ⓓ sad and discouraged

6. The poet probably believes that _____.
- Ⓐ all people should get along
- Ⓑ peace on earth is impossible
- Ⓒ people cannot forgive each other
- Ⓓ people everywhere face challenges

Understanding the Poem

1. The prefix *re-* means "to make or do again." The word *renew* means "to make new again." Write the meaning of these words that have the prefix *-re*.

   rewrite _____

   reappear _____

   review _____

2. The poet could have included punctuation in this poem. Why do you think she left it out?

   _____

   _____

3. Draw a line to connect each word with its meaning.

harmony	**all human beings**
spirit	**a pleasing combination**
humanity	**life force**

4. Remember that when consonant sounds repeat in more than one word, it is called *alliteration*. In "New Year Prayer," four words begin with an *h* sound. What are they?

   _____   _____

   _____   _____

5. In the last line of the poem, the word *humanity* can mean several things. Circle all of the possible meanings below.

   all humans   **all living things**   **human caring**   **compassion**

6. The words in the poem may be read as three phrases. What are they?

   _____

   _____

   _____

Before You Read the Poem

Build Background

Remind students that some of the poems in this unit are about the seasons of the year. Explain that the next poem is by William Carlos Williams, one of the great pioneers of modern free verse. A physician as well as a writer, Dr. Williams was born in Rutherford, New Jersey, in 1883. It is interesting to note that his mother, who had a great influence on his work, was Puerto Rican and spoke Spanish. William Carlos Williams wanted poetry to speak to ordinary people as well as scholars. In "Winter Trees," Williams depicts an early winter woods in the moonlight. The wise trees have prepared for harsh weather by letting go of unnecessary complications: their leaves.

Build Vocabulary

Encourage students to give the meaning for words on this list that are familiar. Provide simple definitions for unfamiliar words.

attiring: dressing

completed: finished

complicated: hard to understand; not simple

disattiring: undressing

liquid: fluid; smooth and unhampered in movement

thus: so; in this way

While You Read the Poem

Invite students to read through the poem silently one or two times. Then read it aloud for them, demonstrating how the line breaks reproduce the cadence of speech. Have the students read the poem aloud as a group; then write it on the board as three ordinary sentences. Have a volunteer read the sentences. Finally, call on students to comment on the difference between the two readings.

After You Read the Poem

Elements of Poetry

Poet's Toolbox: Contrast Work with students to find the words reviewed in the Build Vocabulary section. Point out that all are located in the first seven lines of the poem. The last three lines contain only simple, everyday words. This direct language echoes the message of the last lines, that simplicity is a "wise" survival strategy. The "complicated" language in the first section of the poem helps make this simple conclusion stand out.

Poet's Toolbox: Personification When a poet gives human qualities to nonhuman things, it is called *personification*. Ask students to point out how Williams has personified the trees. (They are capable of "attiring and disattiring"; they have "prepared their buds"; they are "wise" and able to "stand" and "sleep.")

Follow-up Activities

Students may work independently to complete the activities on pages 45 and 46.

Winter Trees

All the complicated details

of the attiring and

the disattiring are completed!

A liquid moon

moves gently among

the long branches.

Thus having prepared their buds

against a sure winter

the wise trees

stand sleeping in the cold.

—William Carlos Williams

Read and Understand Poetry • EMC 3326 • ©2005 by Evan-Moor Corp.

Understanding the Poem

Read each question and choose the best answer. You may wish to reread "Winter Trees" as you work.

1. What season is named in the poem?

Ⓐ fall

Ⓑ winter

Ⓒ spring

Ⓓ summer

2. Which of these is mentioned first in the poem?

Ⓐ a sure winter

Ⓑ tree branches

Ⓒ liquid moonlight

Ⓓ complicated details

3. The word *prepared* probably means _____ .

Ⓐ warmed

Ⓑ destroyed

Ⓒ made ready

Ⓓ covered with wax

4. This poem is <u>not</u> about _____ .

Ⓐ sleeping trees

Ⓑ trees in early spring

Ⓒ preparation for winter

Ⓓ moonlight in tree branches

5. During the winter, these trees will _____ .

Ⓐ die

Ⓑ change

Ⓒ start growing

Ⓓ remain dormant

6. What time of year is shown in the poem?

Ⓐ early winter

Ⓑ late summer

Ⓒ late spring

Ⓓ early fall

Name _____

Understanding the Poem

1. The prefix *-dis* is magic. It can turn a word into its opposite, or antonym. In the poem "Winter Trees," what is the antonym of *attiring?*

_____

If *attiring* means "getting dressed," what does *disattiring* mean?

_____

Now, write antonyms for each of these words:

disagree _____   **discover** _____

discomfort _____   **disharmony** _____

disbelieve _____   **dishonor** _____

disadvantage _____   **dislike** _____

2. Poets sometimes play with language and invent words. Use the prefix *-dis* to invent a word of your own. Write its meaning as well. Follow this example: *disremember: to forget something.*

_____

3. The narrator portrays trees with human qualities when he says they "sleep." Explain what the poet is referring to with this image.

_____

_____

What does the narrator mean when he says the trees are "wise"?

_____

_____

4. Imagine a tree in the springtime. Write a description that gives the tree human qualities, or personifies it.

As the winds blow the ...... stand ... well dressed trees quake with fear

Create another description to personify a tree in the autumn.

The mighty oaks ...... a long queens adorned in their ..... robes and ... crowns.

Outside My Window

Contents

Before You Read the Poem

Build Background

Tell students that the poems in this unit describe scenes from the world outside. The poem they will read next is called "Free as a...." In this poem, the speaker imagines what it would be like to be a bird. Ask students what animal they would like to be for just an hour or a day. Invite them to share imagined experiences as that animal.

While You Read the Poem

Invite students to read through the poem silently one or two times. Then select a volunteer to read it aloud for the class. Have the class notice the position of each punctuation mark. Remind them that punctuation marks are like rests in music, signaling a moment of silence. Have the class read the poem together, pausing at each punctuation mark. Have them think of themselves as a chorus, saying each word together. Explain that this kind of performance is called a *choral reading*. You may wish to model "directing" the performance, or to invite student volunteers to do so.

After You Read the Poem

Elements of Poetry

Form: List Poem Tell students that this poem is written as free verse, so it does not use any special pattern of rhyme or meter. This free verse poem builds its rhythm with lists. The famous American poet Walt Whitman used lists in many of his works. Have the students find a list of things the bird sees from the air, and then ask them to find a list of things the bird does.

Poet's Toolbox: Alliteration Tell students that alliteration is the repetition of initial sounds in words that are close to each other in a text. Invite students to find examples of alliteration in the poem, such as "wild world, wonder." Students will have additional practice with alliteration on the second activity page.

Follow-up Activities

Students may work independently to complete the activities on pages 50 and 51.

Read and Understand Poetry • EMC 3326 • ©2005 by Evan-Moor Corp.

Free as a...

First thing
outside my window
the wild world sings.
I wonder
How it would be
to fly over
my neighborhood,
box houses,
streets like lines
on a map,
tops of trees;
to pull a worm
breakfast from mud
between grass blades;
to build a soft house
for my children
in the branches
of a cottonwood
or to be
such a child
too big for the nest,
taking one wild step
into air.

—Linda Armstrong

Free as a...

Understanding the Poem

Read each question and choose the best answer. You may wish to reread "Free as a…" as you work.

1. This poem is mainly about _____ .
   - Ⓐ pulling worms out of mud
   - Ⓑ streets like lines on a map
   - Ⓒ what it would be like to be a bird
   - Ⓓ looking down on the tops of trees

2. Which of these is <u>not</u> mentioned in the poem?
   - Ⓐ streets
   - Ⓑ a worm
   - Ⓒ birds' eggs
   - Ⓓ a bird's nest

3. Which of these is mentioned first in the poem?
   - Ⓐ a nest
   - Ⓑ a window
   - Ⓒ a baby bird
   - Ⓓ a neighborhood

4. A *cottonwood* is probably a kind of _____ .
   - Ⓐ car
   - Ⓑ tree
   - Ⓒ bird
   - Ⓓ cloth

5. According to this speaker, birds are _____ .
   - Ⓐ free
   - Ⓑ busy
   - Ⓒ confused
   - Ⓓ endangered

6. Which of these would be a good word to put at the end of the poem's title?
   - Ⓐ bird
   - Ⓑ tree
   - Ⓒ map
   - Ⓓ worm

Understanding the Poem

1. The images that the poet includes in "Free as a…" are presented from two different points of view: from a child's perspective and others from a bird's point of view. Read each phrase from the poem. Circle the word that tells the point of view represented in the phrase.

outside my window	bird	child
a worm breakfast	bird	child
tops of trees	bird	child
I wonder	bird	child
streets like lines	bird	child

2. When a poet uses the same beginning sound in words that are close to each other, it is called *alliteration*. Alliteration helps give poems their special sound. List all the examples of alliteration you can find in "Free as a…."

   _____

   _____

3. Who is the "child too big for the nest" mentioned at the end of the poem?

   _____

4. Who is "taking one wild step into air"? Explain this part of the poem.

   _____

5. Tell about a time when you did something for the first time. Did you feel like you were "taking one wild step into air"? Describe what you did and how you felt.

   _____

   _____

6. In this poem, the poet describes things as they would look to a bird. Describe the following as they would look to an ant. The first one has been done for you.

grass	blades of grass like skyscrapers
people	_____
a puddle	_____
a worm	_____
a rock	_____

Before You Read the Poems

Build Background

Remind students that the poems in this unit deal with the outdoors. Explain that the collection of poems they will read next are written in a Japanese form called *haiku*. Matsuo Munefusa, who wrote under the name of Basho, is generally regarded as the master of this poetic form. He lived in Japan from 1644 to 1695. Traditionally, haiku was intended to capture the essence of a moment in nature. Some haiku can also be humorous, and this is especially true of modern haiku. The last poem in the collection, "Hiker," is by a contemporary poet, and it shows how haiku can capture the "humorous moment" in commonplace activities.

While You Read the Poems

Ask individual students to take turns reading each of the poems aloud. Remind students that they don't necessarily have to pause at the end of each line. In some cases, a sentence continues from one line to the next. Haiku is too short to establish a rhythm, and it often sounds like a simple statement when read aloud. Have the class vote for their favorite haiku in the collection, and then read it aloud together.

After You Read the Poems

Elements of Poetry

Form: Haiku Write one of the poems on the board and have students help you determine the number of syllables in each line. Draw a slash after each syllable, showing students that the first and last lines have five syllables, and the second line has seven syllables. Students will have additional practice counting syllables on the second activity page.

Poet's Toolbox: Detail Detail is the soul of haiku. The haiku poet tries to find that single detail that reveals the most important thing about a particular moment, situation, or experience. With students, apply this principle to each poem in the collection. Ask why they think the poet chose those particular details, and what those details reveal about the particular moment described in the poem. Why do they think this moment was worth writing about? Suggest to students that haiku tries to open our eyes to the beauty, humor, and mystery of everyday events. These poems show us that life is made up of details, and that those details are worth paying attention to.

Follow-up Activities

Students may work independently to complete the activities on pages 54 and 55.

Worm

At night, quietly,
a worm under the moonlight
digs into a nut.

—*Basho*

Tulips

Pushing through moist earth
tulips leave no room for doubt:
spring is here at last.

—*Sarita Chávez Silverman*

Lightning Jumpshot

Daddy's voice thunders
he shoots a lightning jumpshot
through a sweaty storm

—*Michael Burgess*

Hiker

Walked five miles today
and seven miles yesterday.
Five more tomorrow.

—*Ian McMillan*

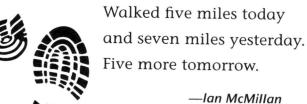

Understanding the Poems

Read each question and choose the best answer. You may wish to reread "Haiku Collection" as you work.

1. Which of these is <u>not</u> mentioned in Basho's haiku?

Ⓐ a nut
Ⓑ sunrise
Ⓒ a worm
Ⓓ moonlight

2. The nut in Basho's poem will _____ .

Ⓐ not be harmed
Ⓑ be buried in a hole
Ⓒ be eaten by the worm
Ⓓ sprout and begin to develop

3. You can tell from "Tulips" that these flowers _____ .

Ⓐ have sharp petals
Ⓑ bloom in the spring
Ⓒ bloom for a very short time
Ⓓ bloom in many bright colors

4. "Lightning Jumpshot" is mainly about _____ .

Ⓐ a father shouting
Ⓑ a dangerous storm
Ⓒ some sweating players
Ⓓ a father playing basketball

5. In "Lightning Jumpshot," *thunders* means _____ .

Ⓐ scares people
Ⓑ sounds angry
Ⓒ breaks windows
Ⓓ is loud and powerful

6. In each line of "Hiker," the number of miles he must walk _____ .

Ⓐ is the same as the number of syllables in the line
Ⓑ rhymes with the end of the next line
Ⓒ equals the total number of miles
Ⓓ is more than the day before

Understanding the Poems

1. **a.** "Hiker" is a humorous haiku. What is funny about the title? If you're not sure, say it aloud to yourself.

   _____

   b. How does the content of "Hiker" refer to the form of haiku itself?

   _____

2. "Lightning Jumpshot" is about basketball, not the traditional nature theme of classic haiku. Read each line again and write the words that show that the poet found a way to include elements of nature in his haiku about a basketball game.

   _____   _____   _____

3. Haiku follows a very precise syllable pattern. Make a slash (/) after each syllable in "Tulips," "Lightning Jumpshot," and "Hiker." Then count the number of syllables in each line and write it in the space provided.

Tulips

Pushing through moist earth   _____

tulips leave no room for doubt: _____

spring is here at last.   _____

Lightning Jumpshot

Daddy's voice thunders   _____

he shoots a lightning jumpshot   _____

through a sweaty storm   _____

Hiker

Walked five miles today   _____

and seven miles yesterday.   _____

Five more tomorrow.   _____

Before You Read the Poem

Build Background

Remind students that the poems in this unit are about scenes in nature. Tell students that the poem they will read next is called "Dust of Snow." In the poem, a crow knocks a little snow down on the speaker, who is in a bad mood. The speaker awakens to his surroundings and cheers up. Invite volunteers to speculate about how an experience in the snow might improve a grouchy mood.

Build Vocabulary

Invite volunteers to share the meaning of the expression to "rue the day." If it is unfamiliar to students, use an example to help them deduce its meaning. You might say, for example: *After Adam broke his arm skating, he said, "I rue the day I bought those skates!"* Make sure students understand that the expression means "to feel regret." Let them know that they will encounter a form of this expression in "Dust of Snow."

While You Read the Poem

Invite students to read through the poem silently one or two times. Then read it aloud for the class. Next, divide the class into two groups. Have one group stand and read the first stanza. Then have the second group stand and read the concluding stanza.

After You Read the Poem

Elements of Poetry

Form: Rhymed Lyric Tell students that this is a rhyming lyric poem. Remind them that in lyric poetry, the poet shares feelings and impressions rather than tells a story, as in a narrative poem. Have volunteers point out rhyming words in the poem, and then work with students to identify the rhyming pattern: *abab cdcd.*

Poet's Toolbox: Meter Explain that meter is a definite rhythm pattern in a poem. When a poem has a metric pattern, each line may be divided into feet. A foot is a rhythmic unit. "Dust of Snow" has two feet in each line. The first foot, "The way," has two beats. The first beat is unstressed. The second beat is stressed. This pattern of stressed meter is called an *iambic foot.* Let students know that it is one of the most common rhythmic patterns in English verse. Have students clap the rhythmic pattern of the poem's first line, clapping louder for the stressed beat. Vocalize the meter using *ta* for unstressed beats and **da** for stressed beats: *ta* **da** *ta* **da**. Help students find other iambic feet in the poem.

Follow-up Activities

Students may work independently to complete the activities on pages 58 and 59.

Dust of Snow

The way a crow
Shook down on me
The dust of snow
From a hemlock tree

Has given my heart
A change of mood
And saved some part
Of a day I had rued.

—*Robert Frost*

Understanding the Poem

Read each question and choose the best answer. You may wish to reread "Dust of Snow" as you work.

1. What kind of tree is mentioned in the poem?
   - (A) a fir
   - (B) a pine
   - (C) a birch
   - (D) a hemlock

2. Which of these is mentioned first in the poem?
   - (A) the tree
   - (B) the crow
   - (C) the speaker's heart
   - (D) the speaker's mood

3. What is a "dust of snow"?
   - (A) a ball of white dust
   - (B) a crushed snowball
   - (C) a light sprinkling of snowflakes
   - (D) pollen dust from a hemlock tree

4. This poem is not about _____.
   - (A) the life of a crow
   - (B) being in a bad mood
   - (C) walking outside in the winter
   - (D) noticing the world around you

5. You can tell from this poem that the crow _____.
   - (A) flew over the hemlock
   - (B) was shaking in the cold
   - (C) was in the hemlock tree
   - (D) had a nest in the hemlock

6. After the dust of snow fell, the speaker felt _____.
   - (A) better
   - (B) trapped
   - (C) miserable
   - (D) disappointed

 Read and Understand Poetry • EMC 3326 • ©2005 by Evan-Moor Corp.

Understanding the Poem

1. The first stanza of "Dust of Snow" introduces two characters. Who are they?

   _____

2. Robert Frost lived in New England and set most of his poems there. Could "Dust of Snow" be set anywhere? Does the setting make a difference in this poem? Explain your answer.

   _____

   _____

3. In painting, putting dark and light colors together creates drama. How did Frost do this in "Dust of Snow"? Read the phrases below. Decide if Frost used each element to create a "light" or a "dark" image. Write the words in the correct column.

a hemlock tree	the speaker's mood before the snow fell	a dust of snow
a crow	the speaker's mood after the snow fell	snow on the ground

light	dark
_____	_____
_____	_____
_____	_____

4. Frost used rhyming words to help shape "Dust of Snow." For each of these words from the poem, write the rhyming word that Frost chose. Then write another rhyming word. Remember, rhyming words don't always have the same spelling pattern.

crow	me	heart	mood
_____	_____	_____	_____
_____	_____	_____	_____

5. In "Dust of Snow," Robert Frost presents a scene from a short moment in time and describes his feelings during that moment. Use your own words in several sentences to describe this moment.

   _____

   _____

   _____

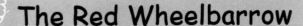

Before You Read the Poem

Build Background

If students have already read "Winter Trees" (see page 44), you might wish to tell them that the poem they will read next is also by American poet William Carlos Williams. This poem, entitled "The Red Wheelbarrow," is actually one sentence. By focusing on one seemingly insignificant subject at one seemingly insignificant moment in time, Williams points out in this poem that nothing is insignificant.

Build Vocabulary

Invite volunteers to say what a *glaze* is, or what it means to *glaze* something. If you need to prompt students, ask if they are familiar with sugar glazes on pies or cakes, or with glazes used in making pottery. If necessary, explain that a glaze is a shiny, translucent liquid that is used to coat something. When something is glazed, it is covered with this type of coating.

While You Read the Poem

Invite students to read through the poem silently one or two times. Remind students that the poem is really one sentence. Encourage them to try pausing in different places as they read, or not pause at all. Have volunteers present a variety of approaches to reading the poem aloud for the class. Encourage the group to decide which approach to reading seems to work best for the poem.

After You Read the Poem

Elements of Poetry

Form: Free Verse Tell students that this poem is written as free verse, so it does not follow a pattern of rhyme. Nevertheless, it is divided into stanzas. Have students identify the number of lines in each stanza. Remind students that some poems, such as haiku, are built around specific syllable patterns. Help students count the number of syllables in each line and note the pattern. Discuss whether the syllable pattern sets a rhythm in the poem. Students will probably agree that it does not. The arrangement of the text, however, does help draw attention to each word. The poet's decision to break apart the compound words *wheelbarrow* and *rainwater* also helps draw attention to each element. Point out that this may be another way that the poet shows us that things that may seem insignificant really are not.

Poet's Toolbox: Capitalization, Punctuation Poets often break the rules of capitalization and punctuation on purpose to achieve a particular effect. Ask students to speculate about why the poet chose to omit these elements from this poem. Ask them to comment on the difference between seeing "The Red Wheelbarrow" and hearing it. You may need to point out how the importance of each seemingly insignificant element is made visible in this written form.

Follow-up Activities

Students may work independently to complete the activities on pages 62 and 63.

The Red Wheelbarrow

so much depends
upon

a red wheel
barrow

glazed with rain
water

beside the white
chickens

—William Carlos Williams

Understanding the Poem

Read each question and choose the best answer. You may wish to reread "The Red Wheelbarrow" as you work.

1. Which of the following is <u>not</u> mentioned in the poem?
- Ⓐ cows
- Ⓑ water
- Ⓒ chickens
- Ⓓ a wheelbarrow

2. Which of these is mentioned first in the poem?
- Ⓐ chickens
- Ⓑ rainwater
- Ⓒ the color white
- Ⓓ a wheelbarrow

3. The word *glazed* probably means _____.
- Ⓐ filled
- Ⓑ rusted
- Ⓒ coated
- Ⓓ polished

4. This poem is <u>not</u> about _____.
- Ⓐ a wet, red wheelbarrow
- Ⓑ farm animals in the rain
- Ⓒ the moments after a rain shower
- Ⓓ a wheelbarrow near some chickens

5. Which of these words would best describe the surface of the wheelbarrow?
- Ⓐ dry
- Ⓑ rusty
- Ⓒ shiny
- Ⓓ muddy

6. You can tell from the poem that there has just been _____.
- Ⓐ a tornado
- Ⓑ a snowstorm
- Ⓒ a rain shower
- Ⓓ an earthquake

Understanding the Poem

1. Write the two-syllable words from the poem below.

_____   _____   _____

_____   _____   _____

2. Which two words would have had three syllables if the poet had not separated them onto two different lines?

_____   _____

3. When two separate words are joined together to form a new word, it is called a *compound word*. In the poem, two compound words are written as four separate words. Write the separate words below, and then write them as compound words.

_____ + _____ = _____

_____ + _____ = _____

4. To identify other compound words, connect a word in the left column with one in the right column. Write the new words below.

sun	road
chalk	water
rail	board
super	ball
under	light
basket	market

_____   _____

_____   _____

_____   _____

5. Look around the room or outside the window for something to describe. Notice the location, color, size, shape, and texture of the object. Using as many descriptive words as you can, write one sentence to describe the object.

_____

6. On the back of this paper, rewrite your sentence so it can be read like a poem. Then share it with a partner.

Before You Read the Poem

Build Background

This poem was written by Alfred, Lord Tennyson, one of the great poets of the English language. In 1850, Tennyson was named poet laureate of England. The tradition of bestowing this title upon a poet of the highest distinction began in England in 1616. The poet laureate seeks to raise an appreciation of poetry throughout the country.

Build Vocabulary

This poem uses some archaic vocabulary. Teach students the meaning of the following words and phrase. Students need not memorize these words because they are not very useful words to know, but they are fun to say and are used by the poet, at least in part, for that very reason.

coot and hern: aquatic birds

cresses: leafy plants that grow near water

fallow: land that is unseeded

foreland: a projecting landmass

grayling: a small fry, or fish

haunt: a favorite place

mallow: a pink flower

sally: a leap forward

thorpe: a hamlet

While You Read the Poem

Different students may read different sections of the poem. If you have at least thirteen students, they may take turns reading individual stanzas. If not, assign two or three stanzas to each student. Help with pronunciation as needed.

After You Read the Poem

Elements of Poetry

Form: Rhyming Verse Help students identify the rhyming pattern in this poem, which is *abab*. Point out that the rhyming pair in the refrain, *river* and *ever*, is a "soft rhyme" because the vowel sound in the last syllable of each word is "closed" by the final *r*. With r-controlled vowels such as these, the rhyme can be strengthened by matching the vowel sound in the next-to-last syllable. A stronger rhyming pair, for example, would have been *river* and *shiver*, or *never* and *ever*. The poet probably concluded that the "soft" rhyming pair *river* and *ever* was strengthened by its repetition throughout the poem.

Poet's Toolbox: Alliteration Alliteration is the appearance of two words in close proximity that start with the same consonant sound. An example is "sudden sally," which appears in the second line of the poem. Ask students to find other examples of alliteration in the poem. Make sure that they include "field and fallow," "men may come," "fairy foreland," "foamy flake," "golden gravel," and "skimming swallows." In addition, students may notice that certain lines such as "I murmur under moon and stars" also contain alliteration, even though the two words starting with the same letter don't appear side by side.

Follow-up Activities

Students may work independently to complete the activities on pages 67 and 68.

The Brook

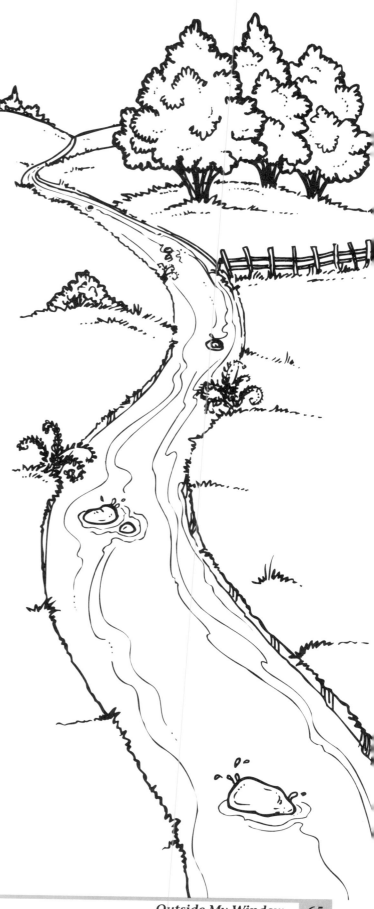

1 I come from haunts of coot and hern,
    I make a sudden sally
    And sparkle out among the fern,
      To bicker down a valley.

2   By thirty hills I hurry down,
     Or slip between the ridges,
    By twenty thorpes, a little town,
     And half a hundred bridges.

3   Till last by Philip's farm I flow
     To join the brimming river,
  For men may come and men may go,
     But I go on for ever.

4   I chatter over stony ways,
     In little sharps and trebles,
    I bubble into eddying bays,
     I babble on the pebbles.

5 With many a curve my banks I fret
     By many a field and fallow,
    And many a fairy foreland set
    With willow-weed and mallow.

6   I chatter, chatter, as I flow
     To join the brimming river,
  For men may come and men may go,
     But I go on for ever.

7   I wind about, and in and out,
With here a blossom sailing,
And here and there a lusty trout,
And here and there a grayling,

8   And here and there a foamy flake
Upon me, as I travel
With many a silvery waterbreak
Above the golden gravel,

9   And draw them all along, and flow
To join the brimming river
For men may come and men may go,
But I go on for ever.

10   I steal by lawns and grassy plots,
I slide by hazel covers;
I move the sweet forget-me-nots
That grow for happy lovers.

11   I slip, I slide, I gloom, I glance,
Among my skimming swallows;
I make the netted sunbeam dance
Against my sandy shallows.

12   I murmur under moon and stars
In brambly wildernesses;
I linger by my shingly bars;
I loiter round my cresses;

13   And out again I curve and flow
To join the brimming river,
For men may come and men may go,
But I go on for ever.

—Alfred, Lord Tennyson

Name _____

Understanding the Poem

Read each question and choose the best answer. You may wish to reread "The Brook" as you work.

1. This poem describes the path of a brook _____.
   - (A) up a mountain
   - (B) through a busy city
   - (C) from its source to its end
   - (D) on its way over a waterfall

2. One of the last places that the brook passes is _____.
   - (A) a wilderness
   - (B) a bridge
   - (C) a farm
   - (D) a lawn

3. When the poet says that the brook "babbles," he's referring to the _____.
   - (A) twists and turns it takes
   - (B) bubbles that rise to its surface
   - (C) way it shines and sparkles in the sun
   - (D) sound it makes as it washes over rocks and stones

4. Look at stanza 12. The poet uses the words *linger* and *loiter* to show how the brook _____.
   - (A) never stops moving
   - (B) can't make up its mind
   - (C) swirls around in circles
   - (D) slows down in some places

5. The poet seems to be saying that nature _____.
   - (A) is more powerful than any machine
   - (B) will go on no matter what people do
   - (C) cannot keep up with the growth of cities
   - (D) can teach us many things if only we would listen

6. Tennyson uses alliteration in "The Brook" to _____.
   - (A) make the poem longer
   - (B) help create a rhyme scheme
   - (C) help add humor to the poem
   - (D) imitate the sounds of flowing water

Understanding the Poem

1. When a poet places more than one word with the same beginning sound close together in a poem, it is called *alliteration*, as in "sudden sally" in the second line of the poem. Write other examples of alliteration from each stanza.

Stanza 1   sudden sally _____

Stanza 2   _____

Stanza 3   _____

Stanza 4   _____

Stanza 5   _____

Stanza 6   _____

Stanza 7   _____

Stanza 8   _____

Stanza 9   _____

Stanza 10 _____

Stanza 11 _____

Stanza 12 _____

Stanza 13 _____

2. This poem tells about the way a brook sounds and moves as it makes its way to the river. Complete the following chart by using words from the poem that describe how water sounds and how it moves. Add words of your own, too.

Water	
Sounds	Movement

3. Using words from the chart, write a sentence about water. The sentence could be about a waterfall, the ocean, or water coming out of a faucet.

_____

_____

_____

War & Peace

Contents

Before You Read the Poem

Build Background

This poem tells the story of a disastrous cavalry charge that took place near the port city of Sevastopol in what is now Ukraine. In 1854, the British and French joined with the Turks to force Russian occupiers out of ports on the Black Sea. The region is called the Crimea, and the war was the Crimean War. Point out the region on a map. Explain that as part of a battle now known as the Battle of Balaclava, a British cavalry unit was ordered to take control of some important hills. According to some historians, of the 673 men who rode into a valley, only 198 survived; they were trapped in the valley under enemy fire.

Build Vocabulary

Encourage students to give meanings for these words and phrase. Explain any that are unfamiliar. Point out that poets sometimes create their own spellings for words; they will see that Tennyson has used 'd for -ed in a number of these words.

blunder'd (blundered): to have made a stupid mistake

dismay'd (dismayed): to have lost courage

league: a unit of measure between two and a half and four and a half miles (no longer in use)

Light Brigade: a unit of fast horse soldiers more often used for scouting and covering retreats than for the kind of fighting encountered at Balaclava

sabre: a special sword with a curved blade used by cavalry, or horse soldiers

sunder'd (sundered): split; forced apart

volley'd (volleyed): shot many weapons off at the same time

While You Read the Poem

Before you read the poem aloud to students, practice reading it to yourself in order to establish the rhythm of the dactylic meter (see below for examples). Then invite students to listen as you read the poem aloud. You may wish to have volunteers each read a stanza aloud for the class. A group of students may wish to prepare a live or videotaped performance of the poem.

After You Read the Poem

Elements of Poetry

Poet's Toolbox: Dactylic Meter Patterns of beats in a line of poetry are called *feet*. A pattern that includes a stressed syllable followed by two unstressed syllables is called a *dactylic foot*. To help students note Tennyson's use of this unusual meter, exaggerate the stress pattern as you read several lines: ***Half*** *a league,* ***half*** *a league,* etc. Note also how the final line in each stanza breaks the pattern of dactylic meter to help mark the end of the stanza. Students may also notice other lines that do not follow the pattern of dactylic meter perfectly.

Follow-up Activities

Students may work independently to complete the activities on pages 73 and 74.

The Charge of the Light Brigade

Memorializing Events in the Battle of Balaclava, October 25, 1854

Written April 10, 1864

1

Half a league, half a league,
Half a league onward,
All in the valley of Death
Rode the six hundred.
'Forward, the Light Brigade!
Charge for the guns!' he said:
Into the valley of Death
Rode the six hundred.

2

'Forward, the Light Brigade!'
Was there a man dismay'd?
Not tho' the soldier knew
Some one had blunder'd:
Their's not to make reply,
Their's not to reason why,
Their's but to do and die:
Into the valley of Death
Rode the six hundred.

3

Cannon to right of them,
Cannon to left of them,
Cannon in front of them
Volley'd and thunder'd;
Storm'd at with shot and shell,
Boldly they rode and well,
Into the jaws of Death,
Into the mouth of Hell
Rode the six hundred.

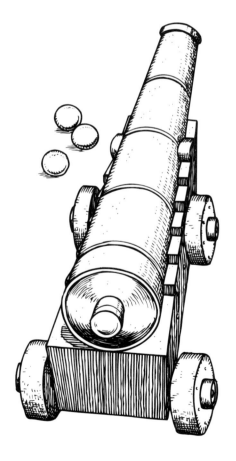
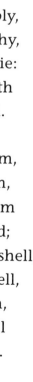

4

Flash'd all their sabres bare,
Flash'd as they turn'd in air
Sabring the gunners there,
Charging an army, while
All the world wonder'd:
Plunged in the battery-smoke
Right thro' the line they broke;
Cossack and Russian
Reel'd from the sabre-stroke
Shatter'd and sunder'd.
Then they rode back, but not
Not the six hundred.

5

Cannon to right of them,
Cannon to left of them,
Cannon behind them
Volley'd and thunder'd;
Storm'd at with shot and shell,
While horse and hero fell,
They that had fought so well
Came thro' the jaws of Death,
Back from the mouth of Hell,
All that was left of them,
Left of six hundred.

6

When can their glory fade?
O the wild charge they made!
All the world wonder'd.
Honour the charge they made!
Honour the Light Brigade,
Noble six hundred!

—*Alfred, Lord Tennyson*

Understanding the Poem

Read each question and choose the best answer. You may wish to reread
"The Charge of the Light Brigade" as you work.

1. Which of these is <u>not</u> mentioned in "The Charge of the Light Brigade"?

   (A) guns
   (B) sabres
   (C) saddles
   (D) cannons

2. Which of these is mentioned first in the poem?

   (A) the valley
   (B) the order
   (C) the cannons
   (D) the six hundred

3. "The Charge of the Light Brigade" is mainly about _____.

   (A) faithful horses in the British army in 1854
   (B) a heroic cavalry charge in the Crimean War
   (C) weapons used by the Russian army in 1854
   (D) cavalrymen who carried lanterns to show the way

4. The word *sabring* in stanza 4 probably means _____.

   (A) encircling the enemy during an attack
   (B) savoring the prospect of a good fight
   (C) attacking someone with a sabre
   (D) ringing the attack bell

5. At the end of the poem, what does the poet ask his listeners to do?

   (A) join the Light Brigade
   (B) honor the Light Brigade
   (C) avoid the same mistakes
   (D) ride into the valley of Death

6. As soon as they rode into the valley, the soldiers knew that they _____.

   (A) would capture the guns
   (B) had the advantage
   (C) were sure to win
   (D) could not win

Understanding the Poem

1. Read each word below. Then write the form used in the poem.

   dismayed _____   through _____

   wondered _____   volleyed _____

   blundered _____   turned _____

2. "The Charge of the Light Brigade" uses rhyme and meter to suggest the hoofbeats of galloping horses. Write rhyming words from the poem on the lines.

   brigade   **blundered**   **reply**   **bare**

   _____   _____   _____   _____

   _____   _____   _____   _____

                      _____

                      _____

3. This poem uses dactylic meter. This pattern of rhythm has a stressed syllable followed by two unstressed syllables, as in "**Half** a league, **half** a league." Show the dactylic meter pattern in these lines from the poem by circling the stressed words or syllables.

   Cannon to right of them

   Cannon to left of them

   Cannon in front of them

4. Why is the "Cannon in front of them" in stanza 3 and the "Cannon behind them" in stanza 5?

   _____

5. What does the Light Brigade leader shout to his troops at the beginning of the poem?

   _____

6. What does Tennyson think about the men who rode in the cavalry charge? What do you think and why?

   _____

   _____

Before You Read the Poem

Build Background

Remind students that the poems in this unit are about war and peace. Tell students that the poem they will read next, "In Flanders Fields," was very popular during World War I. A distinguished Canadian physician named John McCrae wrote it after a friend and former student was killed in battle in western Belgium. At the time, the French, Canadians, British, and Belgians were fighting the Germans, who wanted to capture Paris.

Build Vocabulary

Encourage students to give meanings for these words and phrase. Introduce any that are unfamiliar.

amid: among; in the midst of

break faith with: betray the trust of

Flanders: part of northern Belgium

poppies: red flowers that grow quickly in loose soil (in this case, the churned up dirt of a graveyard)

quarrel: argument

scarce: barely or hardly; rare

While You Read the Poem

Invite students to read through the poem silently one or two times. Next, invite a volunteer to read it aloud to the class. Choose a different volunteer to read each stanza. Finally, read the poem aloud as a group.

After You Read the Poem

Elements of Poetry

Form: Meter Explain that this poem is written in rhymed iambic tetrameter. *Tetra* means "four." There are four poetic measures, or *feet*, in each line. Have the students clap soft-loud, soft-loud, soft-loud, soft-loud to hear the beat. Then read the first line aloud, exaggerating the stressed words or syllables: "In **Flan**ders **Fields** the **pop**pies **blow**." Have them mark the rhyme scheme with letters. It is *aabba, aabc, aabbac*.

Follow-up Activities

Students may work independently to complete the activities on pages 77 and 78.

Students may wish to use the library and Internet to find out more about World War I. Have them find out why Germany wanted to capture Paris. Help students find Canada, Germany, Great Britain, and France on a map of the world. If a map of Belgium is available, encourage them to find Ypres, where the soldiers in the poem were buried. It is in the province of West Flanders, near the French border.

In Flanders Fields

In Flanders Fields the poppies blow
Between the crosses, row on row
That mark our place; and in the sky
The larks, still bravely singing, fly
Scarce heard amid the guns below.

We are the Dead. Short days ago
We lived, felt dawn, saw sunset glow,
Loved and were loved, and now we lie
In Flanders Fields.

Take up our quarrel with the foe:
To you from failing hands we throw
The torch; be yours to hold it high.
If ye break faith with us who die
We shall not sleep, though poppies grow
In Flanders Fields.

—John McCrae

Understanding the Poem

Read each question and choose the best answer. You may wish to reread "In Flanders Fields" as you work.

1. Which of these is <u>not</u> mentioned in the poem?
- Ⓐ poppies
- Ⓑ blood
- Ⓒ larks
- Ⓓ guns

2. Which of these is mentioned first in the poem?
- Ⓐ grave markers
- Ⓑ singing birds
- Ⓒ the quarrel
- Ⓓ the enemy

3. "In Flanders Fields" is mainly about _____ .
- Ⓐ passing a torch from one person to another
- Ⓑ keeping graveyards covered with blooming poppies
- Ⓒ the woes of the dead who are buried in foreign lands
- Ⓓ honoring the dead by winning the war that took their lives

4. The word *foe* probably means _____ .
- Ⓐ king
- Ⓑ friend
- Ⓒ enemy
- Ⓓ weapon

5. Who is speaking in the poem?
- Ⓐ a general who lost an important battle
- Ⓑ soldiers who died in a war
- Ⓒ relatives of dead soldiers
- Ⓓ the winners of a war

6. According to the last stanza, the speaker _____ .
- Ⓐ is still alive
- Ⓑ wants to go home
- Ⓒ wants the war to end
- Ⓓ wants others to win the war

Understanding the Poem

1. While this speaker is talking, is the war still going on, or is it over? Explain how you know this from the words in the poem.

   _____

   _____

2. The last stanza reads "To you from failing hands we throw/The torch." What does that mean?

   _____

   _____

3. List words from the poem that rhyme with these words:

   blow   **sky**

   _____   _____

   _____   _____

   _____   _____

   _____   _____

   _____

   _____

4. Circle the stressed words or syllables in each of these lines:

   In Flanders Fields the poppies blow

   Between the crosses, row on row

   That mark our place; and in the sky

   The larks, still bravely singing, fly

   Scarce heard amid the guns below.

Before You Read the Poem

Build Background
Remind students that the poems in this unit are about war and peace. Tell students that the poem they will read next is called "Grass." The places mentioned in the poem are sites of some of the bloodiest battles in modern history. The poet, Carl Sandburg, suggests that military victories are quickly forgotten. Ask students if they have ever visited a battlefield site. Invite them to share their experiences.

Build Vocabulary
Encourage students to find these places on the map:

Austerlitz: a town in the Czech Republic; the site of Napoleon's greatest victory

Gettysburg: a Civil War battlefield and site of the cemetery where Lincoln delivered the Gettysburg Address

Verdun: a town in France and site of the longest battle in World War I

Waterloo: a town in Belgium and site of Napoleon's final defeat

Ypres: a town in Belgium and a battlefield that was the subject of "In Flanders Fields"

While You Read the Poem
Invite students to read through the poem silently one or two times, then invite a volunteer to read it aloud for the class. Students may enjoy hearing the poem read aloud several times by different readers. Encourage all students who wish to try reading it aloud. Read the poem aloud as a group. Choose a volunteer to read the lines of the railway passenger.

After You Read the Poem

Elements of Poetry
Form: Free Verse "Grass" is written as free verse. It is similar to a list poem and uses repetition very effectively. Invite students to find an action word that is used three times *(pile)*. An entire sentence is repeated in the first half of the poem. Challenge students to find it ("Shovel them under and let me work"). Have students find other repetitions in the poem.

Poet's Toolbox: Vivid Verbs Poems are much shorter than novels, short stories, or even essays. They use just a few words to communicate complex experiences, feelings, and ideas. Every word is important in a poem. Verbs, or action words, are the engine of any piece of writing. Without great verbs, the poem or story will not move. Find all of the verbs in "Grass." Discuss how they help create a mental motion picture.

Follow-up Activities
Students may work independently to complete the activities on pages 81 and 82.

Grass

Pile the bodies high at Austerlitz and Waterloo.
Shovel them under and let me work—
     I am the grass; I cover all.

And pile them high at Gettysburg
And pile them high at Ypres and Verdun.
Shovel them under and let me work.
Two years, ten years, and passengers ask the conductor:
     What place is this?
     Where are we now?

     I am the grass.
     Let me work.

—Carl Sandburg

Understanding the Poem

Read each question and choose the best answer. You may wish to reread "Grass" as you work.

1. Which of these is <u>not</u> mentioned in "Grass"?

  Ⓐ Ypres

  Ⓑ Verdun

  Ⓒ Bull Run

  Ⓓ Gettysburg

2. Which of these is mentioned first?

  Ⓐ Ypres

  Ⓑ Verdun

  Ⓒ Waterloo

  Ⓓ Gettysburg

3. "Grass" is mainly about _____.

  Ⓐ bodies piled high at Gettysburg

  Ⓑ the grass that grows over battlefields

  Ⓒ the cemeteries at Austerlitz and Waterloo

  Ⓓ a railroad conductor talking to passengers

4. The phrase "shovel them under" probably means _____.

  Ⓐ use a shovel to bury them

  Ⓑ bury shovels beside them

  Ⓒ put them under shovels

  Ⓓ give them shovels

5. In this poem, what does the grass seem to express about victories in battle?

  Ⓐ every battle changes the world forever

  Ⓑ victorious soldiers live forever in memory

  Ⓒ people never forget the sites of great battles

  Ⓓ even the greatest battles are forgotten by the living

6. Where are the passengers in the poem?

  Ⓐ in a car

  Ⓑ on a train

  Ⓒ on a plane

  Ⓓ in a stagecoach

Understanding the Poem

1. Who or what is speaking in this poem?

_____

_____

2. War is bloody, noisy, and dramatic. Why does Sandburg choose such a humble, quiet speaker?

_____

_____

_____

3. Sandburg names five places in this poem. What are those places, and why does he include them in this poem?

    a. _____

    b. _____

    c. _____

    d. _____

    e. _____

4. Before you learned about these places, did you know where they were and why they were important?

_____

_____

5. Reread the last two lines of the poem. What is the work that the grass will do?

_____

_____

_____

Before You Read the Poem

Build Background

Remind students that the poems in this unit are about war and peace. Tell students that the poem they will read next is called "The Wall." It is by an Afro-Cuban poet named Nicolás Guillén who was born in 1902. When he was growing up in Cuba, many people tried to make him feel ashamed of his African heritage, but he did not let them break his spirit. During his long and successful career, he wrote many poems and articles about social injustice. In this poem, he suggests that people turn away from violence and evil and embrace peace and friendship.

Build Vocabulary

To help focus students on the idea that walls have a dual purpose—to keep things out and to keep things in—guide students in creating a word map about walls similar to this one.

WALLS			
how they look	**what they do**	**how they make you feel**	**what they're made of**
tall strong thick	separate protect divide defend enclose	protected excluded safe trapped	brick stone cement laws fear

While You Read the Poem

Invite students to read through the poem silently. Then perform it as a responsive reading. Take the part of the leader, reading the introduction, the conclusion, and in between, the lines relating to each visitor (e.g., "Knock, knock . . . A rose and a carnation"). Students read the lines of the decision-maker ("Who's there? . . . Open up the wall!"). Repeat the performance, inviting a volunteer to take the leader's part. You may wish to add percussion instruments such as bells or shakers. If you have native Spanish-speakers or are comfortable reading in Spanish, read the original aloud to feel its rhythm.

After You Read the Poem

Elements of Poetry

Poet's Toolbox: Repetition Point out that this poem is built around repetition. Invite students to find similarities and differences between the first and last stanzas, including phrases that are repeated in the second stanza. Point out the alternating pattern of the commands to "open" and "close." Encourage students to find the way the poet varies this pattern in the third stanza.

Poet's Toolbox: Setting This poem does not tell a complete story with clearly identifiable characters and events. Nevertheless, the poet does give us a feeling for a particular setting. Encourage students to identify words that help create a picture of this place, such as *beach, hill, hummingbird, carnation, rose, myrtle,* and *mint.* Encourage students to say what sort of setting these words suggest. Ask them to compare these images to those created by the words in "Dust of Snow" or "The Red Wheelbarrow."

Follow-up Activities

Students may work independently to complete the activities on pages 86 and 87.

The Wall

To make this wall,
bring me all of the hands:
The blacks, their black hands,
the whites, their hands of white.
Ah,
a wall that runs
from the beach up to the hills,
from the hills down to the beach, yes,
over along the horizon.

"Knock, knock!"
"Who's there?"
"A rose and a carnation..."
"Open up the wall!"
"Knock, knock!"
"Who's there?"
"The colonel's saber..."
"Close up the wall!"
"Knock, knock!"
"Who's there?"
"The dove and the laurel..."
"Open up the wall!"
"Knock, knock!"
"Who's there?"
"The scorpion and the centipede..."
"Close up the wall!"

For the heart of a friend,
open up the wall;
for poison and daggers,
close up the wall;
for myrtle and mint,
open up the wall;
for the fangs of a serpent,
close up the wall;
for the hummingbird on a flower,
open up the wall...

Let us raise up a wall
by joining all the hands;
the blacks, their black hands,
the whites, their hands of white.
A wall that runs
from the beach up to the hills,
from the hills down to the beach, yes,
over along the horizon.

—*Nicolás Guillén*
Translation by Sarita Chávez Silverman

La muralla

Para hacer esta muralla,
tráiganme todas las manos:
Los negros, su manos negras,
los blancos, sus blancas manos.
Ay,
una muralla que vaya
desde la playa hasta el monte,
desde el monte hasta la playa, bien,
allá sobre el horizonte.

—¡Tun, tun!
—¿Quién es?
—Una rosa y un clavel...
—¡Abre la muralla!
—¡Tun, tun!
—¿Quién es?
—El sable del coronel...
—¡Cierra la muralla!
—¡Tun, tun!
—¿Quién es?
—La paloma y el laurel...
—¡Abre la muralla!
—¡Tun, tun!
—¿Quién es?
—El alacrán y el ciempiés...
—¡Cierra la muralla!

Al corazón del amigo,
abre la muralla;
al veneno y al puñal,
cierra la muralla;
al mirto y la yerbabuena,
abre la muralla;
al diente de la serpiente,
cierra la muralla;
al ruiseñor en la flor,
abre la muralla...

Alcemos una muralla
juntando todas las manos;
los negros, sus manos negras,
los blancos, sus blancas manos.
Una muralla que vaya
desde la playa hasta el monte,
desde el monte hasta la playa, bien,
allá sobre el horizonte...

—*Nicolás Guillén*

Name _____

Understanding the Poem

Read each question and choose the best answer. You may wish to reread "The Wall" as you work.

1. Which of these is <u>not</u> mentioned in the poem?
   - Ⓐ myrtle and mint
   - Ⓑ poison and daggers
   - Ⓒ the feast and the table
   - Ⓓ the dove and the laurel

2. Which of these is mentioned first in the poem?
   - Ⓐ hands of white
   - Ⓑ all of the hands
   - Ⓒ the colonel's saber
   - Ⓓ a rose and a carnation

3. A *saber* is probably _____ .
   - Ⓐ a weapon
   - Ⓑ a flower
   - Ⓒ a house
   - Ⓓ a tree

4. This poem is <u>not</u> about _____ .
   - Ⓐ refusing to accept evil
   - Ⓑ getting along with other people
   - Ⓒ a summer holiday at the beach
   - Ⓓ accepting beauty and friendship

5. What does the speaker want us to do?
   - Ⓐ keep everyone outside the wall
   - Ⓑ let the good in but keep out evil
   - Ⓒ keep people away from each other
   - Ⓓ build a stone wall around an island

6. The wall of joined hands is really _____ .
   - Ⓐ a decision not to trust anyone
   - Ⓑ a monument near a beach in Cuba
   - Ⓒ a wall decorated with a pattern of hands
   - Ⓓ a decision to choose good and reject evil

The Wall

Understanding the Poem

1. Words have *denotations*, or direct, literal meanings. They also have *connotations*, or symbolic meanings and associations. Draw lines to match each word in the left column with a connotation in the right column.

scorpion	beauty
dove	fragrance
saber	pain
mint	peace
hummingbird	war

2. In "The Wall," the poet lists things that represent the negative, destructive aspects of life. These are contrasted with those that represent positive, life-giving elements. Create your own list of things that could be used to connote good and evil.

Good   **Evil**

_____   _____

_____   _____

_____   _____

_____   _____

3. "The Wall" includes a call-and-response pattern. A leader chants part of the poem and a group responds with a *refrain*, or repeated line. Which line is repeated five times?

_____

4. List the lines that are repeated four times in the poem.

_____

_____

_____

5. Poems with a lot of repetition are favorites when people are working, sitting around a campfire, or hiking. Why?

_____

_____

Before You Read the Poem

Build Background

The legend recounted in the next poem is an important part of Mexico's cultural heritage. It is at least six hundred years old and explains the founding of the Aztec empire. At its height in the 1500s, the Aztec empire was comprised of almost 6 million people and covered 80,000 square miles. The empire was made possible by the Aztecs' superior agricultural techniques and their drive to dominate neighboring peoples. Aztec culture was very militaristic, demanding absolute loyalty and even sacrifice. These values can be seen in Aztec myths and legends. According to one legend, the Aztecs were guided to the Valley of Mexico by a vision. The Sun God had told them they would find, during their migrations, an eagle perched on a cactus, eating a snake. They were to settle in that very place and build a great nation. The following legend tells how this prophecy came true.

While You Read the Poem

Read the poem aloud for the class. First, ask students to close their eyes. Invite them to visualize the imagery and scenes described as you read the work aloud.

After You Read the Poem

Elements of Poetry

Form: Oral Tradition "The Founding of Mexico in 1325" is a part of Mexico's oral tradition. Virtually every person in Mexico knows this legend; it has been told and retold countless times through the generations. As such, it has no particular author. Songs, poems, and stories about the founding of Mexico were probably first circulated by the Aztecs themselves, or by their descendants. They were recited in Nahuatl, an indigenous language. Later, Spanish *conquistadores,* or conquerors, transcribed this material into Spanish, and now it has been translated into many different languages.

Poet's Toolbox: Symbol A symbol is a person, a place, an object, or an action that stands for something besides itself. A flag, for example, can symbolize a state or a country. The individual images in a flag, in turn, might symbolize important values or events from the country's past. Symbols help to convey meaning in a concise and subtle way. In the legend about the founding of Mexico, for example, there are some very powerful symbols from Aztec culture. The eagle is a prominent symbol, for example, and might represent power or victory, especially since it is perched on high and eating a snake. Encourage students to speculate about what each of these images might symbolize. They will have an opportunity to put their ideas in writing when they complete the second activity page.

Follow-up Activities

Students may work independently to complete the activities on pages 91 and 92.

The Founding of Mexico in 1325

One day, Huitzilopochtli, a mighty god, appeared before
Cuahcohuatl, the leader of the Aztecs, and said:
"Go until you find a wild cactus; and there you shall see
a serene eagle perched tall and proud.
There it eats, there it grooms its feathers,
and this shall make your heart content:
For this is where the heart of our enemy has drowned,
swirling round and round!
And where it fell, you will see among the crags,
in a cave stuffed with reeds and sawgrass,
that a wild cactus has sprouted from our enemy's heart!
That is where we shall live, and that is where we shall rule.
People of every sort will come to pay their respect!
We will conquer all the surrounding peoples
with our arms, our shields, and our might!
The city of Tenochtitlan shall rule forever!
There where the eagle screeches, where it spreads its wings:
the place where it eats and where fish fly,
where snakes burrow in the wild!
That place shall be Mexico!—Tenochtitlan!
and many wonderous things shall take place there!"

Then Cuahcohuatl spoke:
"That is very good, my noble priest!
So shall it be.
I will bring this news to my parents,
and all the tribal elders!"

Huitzilopochtli (wee-tsee-loh-POHCH-tlee) • **Cuahcohuatl** (kwa-COH-wahtl) • **Tenochtitlan** (ten-ohch-teet-LAHN)

And then Cuahcohuatl called a gathering of all the elders
and he told them of the words of Huitzilopochtli.
The Aztec people listened,
and they went among the reeds and sawgrass,
to the edge of the cave.
They came to the place where the wild cactus rose up
from the mouth of the cave, and they saw the eagle
standing serene upon the wild cactus.
There it stood, tossing the remains of what it was eating
into the cave.

The eagle could see the Aztecs long before they even arrived,
And when they came close, it bowed deeply.
Its nest and its throne were lined with the finest feathers:
blue jay, pheasant, and quetzal.
The Aztecs saw the heads of these beautiful birds strewn about;
and their feet, and their bones, were all spread around on the ground.

The god spoke to them and said:
"Ah, Aztec nation, it shall be here: Mexico is here!"
And though they could not see who spoke, they began to weep
and they said, "Happy are we, joyful at last:
we have finally seen where our city shall be!
Let us stop our wandering and rest here, now and forever!"

> —*Anonymous*
> **Adapted from the Spanish version**
> **by Michael Ryall**

Name _____

Understanding the Poem

Read each question and choose the best answer. You may wish to reread "The Founding of Mexico in 1325" as you work.

1. This legend tells how the Aztecs _____ .
   - (A) came to an end
   - (B) fought a war against an enemy
   - (C) settled and began a great empire
   - (D) learned how to farm and make tools

2. Huitzilopochtli told Cuahcohuatl a kind of _____ .
   - (A) warning
   - (B) story with a hidden meaning
   - (C) riddle that he had to figure out
   - (D) prophecy, or vision of the future

3. Tenochtitlan was the original name for _____ .
   - (A) Mexico
   - (B) the Sun God
   - (C) Cuahcohuatl
   - (D) a magical bird

4. In this legend, the eagle probably symbolizes _____ .
   - (A) truth
   - (B) power
   - (C) beauty
   - (D) knowledge

5. You can tell that the Aztec people were _____ .
   - (A) peaceful
   - (B) forever wandering
   - (C) aggressive and warlike
   - (D) only concerned with practical matters

6. You can tell from this poem that the Aztecs _____ .
   - (A) cultivated reeds and sawgrass
   - (B) honored parents and elders
   - (C) believed in flying fish
   - (D) hunted pheasants

Name _____

Understanding the Poem

A symbol is a picture that represents, or stands for, something else. The Mexican flag contains many of the same symbols from the legend that you just read. Study the symbols. In the space below, write a short paragraph about the symbols in the Mexican flag. You may wish to color the flag using the colors indicated. Then guess what the colors might symbolize.

red   white   green

_____
_____
_____
_____
_____
_____
_____
_____
_____
_____

Before You Read the Poem

Build Background

In the previous lesson, students read an account of the founding of Mexico from an ancient oral tradition. In this poem, students will read about the destruction of the Aztec empire, as seen through the eyes of the Aztecs themselves. The Aztecs had a rich and beautiful poetic tradition. An elite class of scribes recorded their poems in accordion-style books that were made out of animal skin or fig bark. Today these books are referred to as *codices,* and they are an important source of information about Aztec history because they contain deeds, tributes, biographies, and many other kinds of historical records. After the conquest of Tenochtitlán in 1519, Spaniards systematically burned the Aztecs' vast libraries, partly out of fear of what they contained. Indeed, the depictions of Aztec life in the codices contrasted sharply with versions told by Spanish conquistadores. Only six hundred codices have survived, and some of them tell about the Conquest. This poem tells about the fall of the Aztec city of Tlatelolco. It was originally written in Nahuatl, the language of the Aztecs, and then translated into Spanish. The English version has been prepared especially for this book.

While You Read the Poem

Read the poem aloud for students in an appropriately solemn tone. When you are finished, invite volunteers to take turns reading it aloud for the class.

After You Read the Poem

Elements of Poetry

Form: Elegy An elegy is normally meant to mourn the death of a person; in some cases, as in this poem, an elegy can express sorrow over the destruction of a culture or civilization. Ask students how the poet expresses his grief over the destruction of Tlatelolco. They might notice, for example, that the eating of wood, lizards, and other scraps of food shows how far the once-mighty Aztec nation had fallen; and in the closing, the poet conveys the feeling that he and his people are aware of the great historical importance of this loss.

Poet's Toolbox: Parallel Syntax Parallel syntax is the use of similar grammatical constructions to express ideas that are related or equal in importance. In each stanza of this poem, the sentences, or lines in the stanza, are constructed in a similar way. In the first stanza, for example, the predominant grammatical structure is the passive tense. The last two lines of the second stanza are in the simple present, and the third stanza is characterized by the use of action verbs. Ask students to make similar kinds of observations about other couplets and stanzas in the poem.

Follow-up Activities

Students may work independently to complete the activities on pages 95 and 96.

The Destruction of Tlatelolco

In the road lie broken arrows;
We have torn our hair in grief.
The roofs are gone from our houses;
Their walls are sullied and stained.

Worms are writhing in the streets and plazas;
The walkways are littered with destruction.
Red is the water, like a river of dye;
It has the taste of salt and rust.

In despair we beat our hands against the walls,
and they crumble into bits and pieces.
Our shields protected us in war,
but they cannot save us from our grief.

For bread we chew dry twigs and wood,
We fill our mouths with dirt and mud.
We have eaten anything and everything:
Lizards, mice, and even worms.

Let us gather 'round and mourn
these events my friends,
mourn the end of the Aztec Nation.

The water has become bitter, withered is the land!
The Giver of Life has taken all from Tlatelolco.

—*Anonymous*
**Adapted from the Spanish version
by Michael Ryall**

Read and Understand Poetry • EMC 3326 • ©2005 by Evan-Moor Corp.

Understanding the Poem

Read each question and choose the best answer. You may wish to reread "The Destruction of Tlatelolco" as you work.

1. This poem conveys the poet's sense of _____

   Ⓐ awe

   Ⓑ grief

   Ⓒ anger

   Ⓓ surprise

2. The water must taste like salt and rust because _____ .

   Ⓐ everything tastes bitter

   Ⓑ the wells have all gone dry

   Ⓒ the rivers are polluted with dye

   Ⓓ it is full of blood and abandoned weapons

3. You can tell from the poem that the end of the Aztec nation was brought about by _____ .

   Ⓐ war

   Ⓑ disease

   Ⓒ poor leadership

   Ⓓ drastic changes in the weather

4. In the fifth stanza, what is the meaning of the word *mourn*?

   Ⓐ get revenge

   Ⓑ come together in a group

   Ⓒ tell about a series of events

   Ⓓ weep and wail over the end of something

5. In the last line, who or what is "The Giver of Life"?

   Ⓐ death

   Ⓑ an Aztec god

   Ⓒ the Aztec nation

   Ⓓ the city of Tlatelolco

6. Which of the following is <u>not</u> a way the Aztecs express grief?

   Ⓐ tearing out their hair

   Ⓑ pounding on the walls

   Ⓒ writhing in the plazas

   Ⓓ gathering together to mourn

Understanding the Poem

1. The poem alternates between using verbs in the active tense and in the passive tense. See if you can do the same. Change each sentence into the passive tense. Follow the example.

Active Tense	Passive Tense
We have torn our hair in grief.	Our hair is torn in grief.
We beat our hands against the walls.	
Our shields protected us in war.	
For bread we chew dry twigs and wood.	
We fill our mouths with dirt and mud.	

2. Next to each word, write the number that goes with its meaning.

   a. _____ writhing   1. great sadness

   b. _____ despair   2. dried up

   c. _____ dye   3. loss of all hope

   d. _____ grief   4. tasting sharp and harsh

   e. _____ bitter   5. tint or ink

   f. _____ withered   6. twisting and turning

3. Use each word in a sentence.

   writhing: _____

   despair: _____

   dye: _____

   grief: _____

   bitter: _____

   withered: _____

Mirth & Magic

Contents

Before You Read the Poem

Build Background

Tell students that the poems in this unit are about fanciful and magical subjects. The poem they will read next, "The Great Selkie of Skule Skerry," was originally written to be sung as a ballad, or a story told in song. This ballad was collected in the late 1800s by the famous folklorist Francis J. Child, who studied English and Scottish oral traditions. Many of the works he collected have been sung for over 500 years! This ballad came from the Orkney Islands (located north of Scotland). It tells the story of a young woman who meets a mythical creature called a *selkie*; in the water, a selkie looks like a seal, but on land, it takes a human form. Students may be familiar with this lore from the popular 1995 movie by director John Sayles, *The Secret of Roan Inish*. If so, they may wish to share what they know about selkies.

Build Vocabulary

Encourage students to give meanings for these words and phrases. Introduce any that are unfamiliar.

lass: girl

maiden: unmarried woman; young woman; girl

Orkney Isles: a group of about seventy islands off the northern tip of Scotland

skerry: a small, low-lying islet, often covered with grass

Skule Skerry: an uninhabited island in the Orkney archipelago

selkie (also called a *finn* or *silkie*): an imaginary creature who takes the form of a seal in the sea, but removes the sealskin to appear human on land

While You Read the Poem

Remind students that this poem was actually written to tell a story in song. Invite them to relax and listen to the story as you read the ballad aloud. Observe the punctuation in the text, but be sure to also gently emphasize the rhyming pattern as you read. On another reading, you might have students read the fourth line in each stanza as a repeating refrain that varies slightly each time.

After You Read the Poem

Elements of Poetry

Form: Ballad Remind students that this poem is a ballad. It was composed to be sung, and tells a story. Invite students to retell the story in their own words.

Poet's Toolbox: Rhyme Like most ballads, this one has a regular rhyme scheme. This helps make it easier to remember the words, which is especially important because ballads are transmitted orally. Have partners discover the rhyme scheme by assigning the same letter to lines that end with the same sound. Have students share their findings, which should be *aabb, ccbb, ddbb, eebb, ffbb*.

Follow-up Activities

Students may work independently to complete the activities on pages 100 and 101.

The Great Selkie of Skule Skerry

The selkie be a creature strange.
He rises from the sea to change
To human form, a weird one he,
When home it is in Skule Skerry.

When he be man, he wants to wed.
But still, the sea remains his bed.
Ladies, beware of him who be
A selkie come from Skule Skerry.

His love he wants them to accept,
But ne'er has he a promise kept.
Who is this strange one that they see?
'Tis Selkie come from Skule Skerry.

A maiden from the Orkney Isles,
A target for his charm, his smiles,
Eager for love, no fool was she,
She knew the secret of Skule Skerry.

And so, while Selkie kissed the lass,
She rubbed his neck with Orkney grass.
This had the magic power, you see,
To banish him from Skule Skerry.

—*Traditional*

Understanding the Poem

Read each question and choose the best answer. You may wish to reread
"The Great Selkie of Skule Skerry" as you work.

1. Which of these is <u>not</u> mentioned in the poem?
   - Ⓐ a seal
   - Ⓑ the sea
   - Ⓒ a selkie
   - Ⓓ the Orkney Isles

2. Which of these is mentioned first in the poem?
   - Ⓐ Orkney grass
   - Ⓑ a strange creature
   - Ⓒ his charm and smiles
   - Ⓓ the secret of Skule Skerry

3. The word *ne'er* probably means _____ .
   - Ⓐ near
   - Ⓑ never
   - Ⓒ neither
   - Ⓓ neighbor

4. Why does the ballad warn ladies about the selkie?
   - Ⓐ because ladies are foolish
   - Ⓑ because he's not what he appears to be
   - Ⓒ because he might give them Orkney grass
   - Ⓓ because he'll take them home to Skule Skerry

5. According to this ballad, which of these statements is true?
   - Ⓐ A selkie is honest.
   - Ⓑ A selkie avoids girls.
   - Ⓒ A selkie can change forms.
   - Ⓓ A selkie lives in the mountains.

6. The girl in this version of the ballad _____ .
   - Ⓐ was fooled by the selkie
   - Ⓑ was saved by her brothers
   - Ⓒ used magic to outwit the selkie
   - Ⓓ used Orkney grass to tie up the selkie

Understanding the Poem

1. Sometimes phrases in old poems or ballads are hard to understand because language changes over the years. Singers may also change the words in a ballad, then rearrange their order to fit the pattern of rhyme or rhythm. Read the following phrases, and then write the phrase from the poem with the same meaning.

   he is a weird one _____

   when he is a man _____

   he has never kept a promise _____

   she was not foolish _____

   the selkie is a strange creature _____

2. "The Great Selkie of Skule Skerry" has many rhyming words. For each of these words from the ballad, write a rhyming word from the poem and another rhyming word of your own.

strange	accept	isles
_____	_____	_____
_____	_____	_____
he	**lass**	**bed**
_____	_____	_____
_____	_____	_____

3. Share some information about another kind of imaginary creature believed to live in the sea. Describe the way it looks and acts, and any other information you wish to share.

   _____

   _____

   _____

4. This song is from an oral tradition in the British Isles that goes back hundreds of years. Describe a time and a place where this song might have been sung. Who might have sung it? Who was listening? Was the purpose to entertain, to teach, to scare, or something else? Use your imagination and write what you think on the back of this page.

Before You Read the Poem

Build Background

Remind students that some of the poems in this unit are about mirth, or merriment. Tell students that the poem they will read next is called "You Are Old, Father William." It is from the famous novel *Alice's Adventures in Wonderland* by Charles Dodgson, better known by his pen name, Lewis Carroll. In the poem, the author parodies a poem that was well known during his lifetime. That poem, "The Old Man's Comforts" by Robert Southey, featured Father William's preachy advice on how to stay fit and healthy throughout life. You may wish to compare "You Are Old, Father William" to Southey's poem, which is found online at the following site: http://www.theotherpages.org.

Build Vocabulary

Encourage students to give meanings for these words and phrase. Introduce any that are unfamiliar.

give yourself airs: to pose, brag, or act as if you are better than everybody else

incessantly: without stopping; constantly

injure: harm

limbs: arms and legs

locks: hair

sage: old, wise person

shilling: a British coin no longer in use

suet: solid fat from a cooked animal, used like oil for cooking

supple: flexible

uncommonly: unusually

While You Read the Poem

Invite students to read through the poem silently one or two times, then try a variety of choral reading approaches. Two volunteers might read it aloud for the class: one takes the part of the old man, and the other takes the part of the son. Likewise, assign the father's role to one half of the class, and the son's to the other. Or, read the old man's part yourself and have the class read the son's part.

After You Read the Poem

Elements of Poetry

Form: Parody Explain that a parody is a work that copies the form (and sometimes the content) of an existing piece in order to make fun of it. Encourage students to brainstorm parodies they have heard, such as "On Top of Spaghetti" (a parody of "On Top of Old Smoky"), or any of the humorous songs by parodist extraordinaire "Weird Al" Yankovic.

Poet's Toolbox: Dialog Poets often use dialog to bring different speakers into a poem. Such poems do not always include quotation marks or other identifiers of the speaker. Ask students to point out the elements of dialog in this poem that appear just as they would in dialog set in a prose selection.

Follow-up Activities

Students may work independently to complete the activities on pages 104 and 105.

You Are Old, Father William

"You are old, Father William," the young man said,
    "And your hair has become very white;
And yet you incessantly stand on your head—
    Do you think, at your age, it is right?"

"In my youth," Father William replied to his son,
    "I feared it would injure the brain;
But now that I'm perfectly sure I have none,
    Why, I do it again and again."

"You are old," said the youth, "as I mentioned before,
    And have grown most uncommonly fat;
Yet you turned a back-somersault in at the door—
    Pray, what is the reason of that?"

"In my youth," said the sage, as he shook his grey locks,
    "I kept all my limbs very supple
By the use of this ointment—one shilling the box—
    Allow me to sell you a couple."

"You are old," said the youth, "and your jaws are too weak
    For anything tougher than suet;
Yet you finished the goose, with the bones and the beak—
    Pray, how did you manage to do it?"

"In my youth," said his father, "I took to the law,
    And argued each case with my wife;
And the muscular strength, which it gave to my jaw,
    Has lasted the rest of my life."

"You are old," said the youth, "one would hardly suppose
    That your eye was as steady as ever;
Yet you balanced an eel on the end of your nose—
    What made you so awfully clever?"

"I have answered three questions, and that is enough,"
    Said his father; "don't give yourself airs!
Do you think I can listen all day to such stuff?
    Be off, or I'll kick you down stairs!"

—*Lewis Carroll*

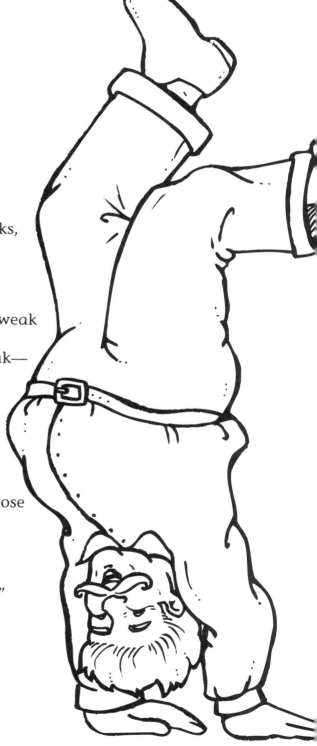

Name _____

You Are Old, Father William

Understanding the Poem

Read each question and choose the best answer. You may wish to reread
"You Are Old, Father William" as you work.

1. Which of the following is <u>not</u> mentioned by Father William?
- Ⓐ his jaw
- Ⓑ his hair
- Ⓒ his brain
- Ⓓ his hearing

2. Which of these is mentioned first in the poem?
- Ⓐ the law
- Ⓑ white hair
- Ⓒ the goose
- Ⓓ a back-somersault

3. "Ointment" is probably _____ .
- Ⓐ fertilizer for trees
- Ⓑ an item of clothing
- Ⓒ something you eat
- Ⓓ something you rub on your skin

4. This poem is mainly about _____ .
- Ⓐ a silly conversation between a father and son
- Ⓑ eating a goose, including the bones and beak
- Ⓒ turning back-somersaults at the door
- Ⓓ standing on your head all the time

5. According to the poem, which of these is probably true?
- Ⓐ Father William is very thin.
- Ⓑ Father William used to be a lawyer.
- Ⓒ Father William loves to answer questions.
- Ⓓ Father William can balance a spoon on his nose.

6. This poem is meant to be _____ .
- Ⓐ mournful
- Ⓑ convincing
- Ⓒ humorous
- Ⓓ informative

104 *Mirth & Magic*   Read and Understand Poetry • EMC 3326 • ©2005 by Evan-Moor Corp.

Understanding the Poem

1. Synonyms are words that have the same meanings. Write the letter for the correct synonym next to each word.

_____	incessantly	a. unusually
_____	injure	b. think
_____	uncommonly	c. flexible
_____	locks	d. smart
_____	supple	e. constantly
_____	couple	f. hair
_____	suet	g. hurt
_____	clever	h. fat
_____	suppose	i. two

2. "You Are Old, Father William" has many rhyming words. Write a rhyming word from the poem on each line, and then add another word of your own.

said	white	son	fat	supple
_____	_____	_____	_____	_____
_____	_____	_____	_____	_____

locks	before	brain	do it	law
_____	_____	_____	_____	_____
_____	_____	_____	_____	_____

3. Write three strange things the father does in this poem.

_____

_____

_____

_____

Before You Read the Poem

Build Background

Remind students that the poems in this unit are about mirth and magic, and that the poem they will read next is called "How Pleasant to Know Mr. Lear," by Edward Lear. Students may already be familiar with Lear's limericks, or his poem "The Owl and the Pussycat." They may be interested to know that Edward Lear was the twentieth child in his family. When his father lost his money on the London stock exchange, Edward was sent to live with his older sister who oversaw his education. Although he is now known as a writer, he made his living as an artist and a drawing teacher. He even instructed Queen Victoria in drawing!

Build Vocabulary

Encourage students to give meanings for these words and phrases. Introduce any that are unfamiliar.

clerical: members of the clergy; priests, ministers, etc.

concrete: opposite of abstract; real; solid; practical; down-to-earth

fastidious: orderly; excessively clean and neat

ill-tempered: grumpy; irritable

laymen: men who are not members of the clergy

pleasant: pleasing; nice

queer: odd; unusual

reckon: count

spherical: round as a ball

tipsy: slightly inebriated, or drunk

visage: face; expression

While You Read the Poem

Read the poem aloud for students. Then assign each stanza to two or three students. After groups practice, have them read the poem aloud.

After You Read the Poem

Elements of Poetry

Poet's Toolbox: Enjambement When a poet finishes a thought by the end of a line, we say the line has an *end stop*. When the thought continues into the next line, it is called an *enjambement*. Point out that most lines in this poem have end stops, but "night-/Gown" is an example of enjambement, used to fit the rhythm and rhyme pattern.

Poet's Toolbox: Invented Words Poets enjoy playing with language. Many poets, including Lewis Carroll and Edward Lear, have created original words. Lear used the invented word *runcible* in several poems. In "The Owl and the Pussycat," there is a runcible spoon, but what is a runcible hat? Nobody is certain. You may wish to encourage creativity with a class "Runcible Hat" show!

Follow-up Activities

Students may work independently to complete the activities on pages 108 and 109.

How Pleasant to Know Mr. Lear

How pleasant to know Mr. Lear,
Who has written such volumes of stuff!
Some think him ill-tempered and queer,
But a few think him pleasant enough.

His mind is concrete and fastidious,
His nose is remarkably big;
His visage is more or less hideous,
His beard it resembles a wig.

He has ears, and two eyes, and ten fingers,
Leastways if you reckon two thumbs;
Long ago he was one of the singers,
But now he is one of the dumbs.

He sits in a beautiful parlour,
With hundreds of books on the wall;
He drinks a great deal of Marsala,
But never gets tipsy at all.

He has many friends, laymen and clerical,
Old Foss is the name of his cat;
His body is perfectly spherical,
He weareth a runcible hat.

When he walks in waterproof white,
The children run after him so!
Calling out, "He's gone out in his night-
Gown, that crazy old Englishman, oh!"

He weeps by the side of the ocean,
He weeps on the top of the hill;
He purchases pancakes and lotion,
And chocolate shrimps from the mill.

He reads, but he does not speak, Spanish,
He cannot abide ginger beer;
Ere the days of his pilgrimage vanish,
How pleasant to know Mr. Lear!

—Edward Lear

Understanding the Poem

Read each question and choose the best answer. You may wish to reread
"How Pleasant to Know Mr. Lear" as you work.

1. Which of these is <u>not</u> mentioned in the poem?
   - (A) a ring
   - (B) books
   - (C) the ocean
   - (D) pancakes

2. Which of these is mentioned first in the poem?
   - (A) his nose
   - (B) a parlour
   - (C) ginger beer
   - (D) chocolate shrimps

3. A *parlour* is probably _____.
   - (A) a car
   - (B) a room
   - (C) a game
   - (D) an animal

4. This poem is mainly about _____.
   - (A) reading Spanish
   - (B) a runcible hat
   - (C) Mr. Lear
   - (D) Old Foss

5. According to the speaker, which of these is true?
   - (A) Mr. Lear is boring.
   - (B) Mr. Lear is very handsome.
   - (C) Mr. Lear is serious and important.
   - (D) Mr. Lear is imperfect, but fun to know.

6. According to the poem, Mr. Lear _____.
   - (A) has many friends
   - (B) is always working
   - (C) is always alone
   - (D) speaks Spanish

Name _____

Understanding the Poem

1. Synonyms are words that have similar meanings. Draw a line from each word to its synonym.

pleasant	face
concrete	careful
tipsy	nice
spherical	practical
ill-tempered	count
fastidious	drunk
visage	grouchy
reckon	round

2. Edward Lear invented the adjective *runcible.* Invent adjectives of your own to match the following meanings, and be sure they work to complete the phrase.

reddish orange: a _____ sunset

worn-out: a _____ sweater

math-loving: a _____ student

joke-loving: a _____ poet

3. When a poet continues the same thought from one line to the next, it is called *enjambement.* When the thought ends at the end of the line, it has an *end stop.* Circle the type of ending for these pairs of lines from different poems.

His mind is concrete and fastidious, His nose is remarkably big.	enjambement end stop
When he be man, he wants to wed. But still, the sea remains his bed.	enjambement end stop
Calling out, "He's gone out in his night- Gown, that crazy old Englishman, oh!"	enjambement end stop
Who is this strange one that they see? 'Tis Selkie come from Skule Skerry.	enjambement end stop

Before You Read the Poem

Build Background

Remind students that the poems in this unit are about mirth and magic. The poem they will read next is called "Two Old Crows," by the American poet Vachel Lindsay. Lindsay lived from 1879 to 1931. He used to go out on long walking tours, exchanging poetry for food and shelter. People loved to hear him read his work aloud. He borrowed rhythms from jazz, chants, and the repetitive cadences of skillful preachers. Tell students that sounds, word games, and humor are all important elements in this poem.

Build Vocabulary

Encourage students to give meanings for these words. Teach any that are unfamiliar.

cause: make something happen

fiddle: violin

mutter: speak softly and unclearly, usually complaining

pale: white; light-colored

stutter: stammer; repeat beginning sounds of words

While You Read the Poem

Encourage students to read the poem silently one or two times. Read the first line aloud, and then encourage the class to read the echo. Continue to read, inviting students to join in on each echoing line. Students may enjoy hearing this poem read aloud several times by different pairs of readers.

After You Read the Poem

Elements of Poetry

Form: Dialog Poets can use dialog just as writers of prose do: to help tell a story. Review with students the words in quotations in this poem to make sure that everyone is clear about who is muttering, stuttering, or buzzing throughout the poem. Encourage students to summarize the story told in this poem, to explain the muttering crow's joke, and to point out other humorous elements in the poem.

Poet's Toolbox: Onomatopoeia Remind students that when words sound like the thing they name, it is called *onomatopoeia*. Ask students to find examples of onomatopoeia in "Two Old Crows" and brainstorm other examples. If your class includes students who speak languages other than English, encourage them to share the words for animal sounds in those languages. Notice whether they also use onomatopoeia.

Follow-up Activities

Students may work independently to complete the activities on pages 112 and 113.

Read and Understand Poetry • EMC 3326 • ©2005 by Evan-Moor Corp.

Two Old Crows

Two old crows sat on a fence rail.
Two old crows sat on a fence rail,
Thinking of effect and cause,
Of weeds and flowers,
And nature's laws.
One of them muttered, one of them stuttered,
One of them stuttered, one of them muttered.
Each of them thought far more than he uttered.
One crow asked the other crow a riddle.
One crow asked the other crow a riddle:
The muttering crow
Asked the stuttering crow,
"Why does a bee have a sword to his fiddle?
Why does a bee have a sword to his fiddle?"
"Bee-cause," said the other crow,
"Bee-cause,
B B B B B B B B B B B B B B B B B-cause."

Just then a bee flew close to their rail:—
"Buzzzzzzzzzz   zzzzzzzz   zzzzzzzz ZZZZZZZ."
And those two black crows
Turned pale,
And away those crows did sail.
Why?
B B B B B B B B B B B B B B B B B-cause.
B B B B B B B B B B B B B B B B B-cause.
"Buzzzzzzzzzz   zzzzzzzz   zzzzzzzz ZZZZZZZ."

—*Vachel Lindsay*

Understanding the Poem

Read each question and choose the best answer. You may wish to reread "Two Old Crows" as you work.

1. Which of these is <u>not</u> mentioned in the poem?
- Ⓐ a bee
- Ⓑ a riddle
- Ⓒ a sword
- Ⓓ a hunter

2. Which of these is mentioned first in the poem?
- Ⓐ a bee
- Ⓑ weeds
- Ⓒ a violin
- Ⓓ a fence rail

3. The word *uttered* probably means _____.
- Ⓐ flew
- Ⓑ walked
- Ⓒ said
- Ⓓ tried

4. This poem is mainly about _____.
- Ⓐ stuttering and muttering
- Ⓑ two crows and a bee
- Ⓒ weeds and flowers
- Ⓓ a fence rail

5. You can tell from the poem that _____.
- Ⓐ the stuttering crow had a sword
- Ⓑ the muttering crow scared the bee
- Ⓒ the bee caused the crows to fly away
- Ⓓ the crows caused the bee to fly away

6. Why did the crow say, "BBBBBBBBBBBBBBBB-cause"?
- Ⓐ He uttered.
- Ⓑ He fiddled.
- Ⓒ He stuttered.
- Ⓓ He muttered.

Name _____

Understanding the Poem

1. Write four lines that are repeated in "Two Old Crows."

   _____

   _____

   _____

   _____

   _____

2. What were the crows thinking about before one of them asked the riddle?

   _____

3. Think about the joke told by the muttering crow. If the bee's "fiddle" refers to the bee's buzzing sound, what is the bee's "sword"? Explain.

   _____

   _____

4. When writers use human characteristics to describe nonhuman things, it is called *personification*. How does the poet personify the crows in this poem?

   _____

   _____

5. Write some examples of onomatopoeia from this poem.

   _____

   _____

6. Now, write some other examples of onomatopoeia.

   _____

   _____

Mirth & Magic   **113**

Before You Read the Poem

Build Background

Remind students that the poems in this unit are about mirth and magic. Tell students that the next selection is an excerpt from William Shakespeare's famous play, *Macbeth*, which is written in verse. Let students know that the play revolves around the intrigue and murder that Macbeth uses to ascend to the throne of Scotland. This excerpt is set in a dark cave where three witches are gathered around a boiling caldron, awaiting Macbeth's arrival. They cast a spell to conjure up a vision of the future to show Macbeth. Many students will probably recognize the now-classic formula used by Shakespeare for the witches' chant.

Build Vocabulary

Remind students that the English language has changed quite a bit since Shakespeare's time. Review the meaning of any unfamiliar words.

adder: a very poisonous snake

broth: a thin soup made by boiling meat, fish, or vegetables

caldron: a kettle or pot

charmed: enchanted

entrails: internal organs; intestines

fenny: from the fens, which are marshy lowlands

fillet: a strip of meat without bones

howlet: a baby owl

newt: a small amphibian with a tail

sweltered: (an archaic definition) exuded; oozed out; gave off

venom: poison, usually injected in a bite

While You Read the Poem

After reviewing the poem yourself, read it aloud for the class in order to help bring meaning to the unfamiliar language. (Note: You need not read the words identifying the speakers.) Invite groups of three students to practice reading the poem together, each taking one witch's part. Encourage groups to take turns presenting their readings to the class.

After You Read the Poem

Elements of Poetry

Form: List Poem This poem is a list of the ingredients that the three wicked old sisters use to mix a magical potion in their caldron. Invite students to name each of the items, restating them in more familiar language as appropriate.

Poet's Toolbox: Alliteration Remind students that when poets place words with the same beginning consonant sound in close proximity in a poem, they are creating alliteration. In this poem, alliteration helps strengthen the singsong quality of the witches' chant. Encourage students to point out examples of alliteration in the text.

Follow-up Activities

Students may work independently to complete the activities on pages 116 and 117.

Round about the caldron go

First Witch

Round about the caldron go;
In the poison'd entrails throw.—
Toad, that under cold stone,
Days and nights has thirty-one;
Swelter'd venom sleeping got,
Boil thou first i' the charmed pot!

All

Double, double, toil and trouble;
Fire, burn; and caldron, bubble.

Second Witch

Fillet of a fenny snake,
In the caldron boil and bake;
Eye of newt, and toe of frog,
Wool of bat, and tongue of dog,
Adder's fork, and blind-worm's sting,
Lizard's leg, and howlet's wing,—
For a charm of powerful trouble,
Like a hell-broth boil and bubble.

All

Double, double, toil and trouble;
Fire, burn; and caldron, bubble.

—*William Shakespeare*
**an excerpt from *Macbeth*
from Act IV, Scene 1**

Name _____

Understanding the Poem

Read each question and choose the best answer. You may wish to reread the excerpt from *Macbeth* as you work.

1. Which of these is <u>not</u> mentioned in the poem?
- Ⓐ lizard's leg
- Ⓑ claw of cat
- Ⓒ adder's fork
- Ⓓ tongue of dog

2. Which of these is mentioned first in the poem?
- Ⓐ a bat
- Ⓑ a toad
- Ⓒ a lizard
- Ⓓ a snake

3. What is the "adder's fork"?
- Ⓐ an intersection of two roads
- Ⓑ an implement for eating
- Ⓒ a snake's tongue
- Ⓓ a poisonous plant

4. This poem is mainly about _____.
- Ⓐ how to kill a king
- Ⓑ creating a powerful charm
- Ⓒ a toad that has slept under a stone
- Ⓓ the eye of a newt and the toe of a frog

5. In this poem, *charm* probably means _____.
- Ⓐ a spell
- Ⓑ delight
- Ⓒ a silver heart
- Ⓓ attractiveness

6. You can <u>not</u> tell from the poem whether the _____ came from an animal.
- Ⓐ toe
- Ⓑ wing
- Ⓒ tongue
- Ⓓ entrails

Name _____

Understanding the Poem

1. Match each of these words used by Shakespeare to its synonym:

caldron	baby owl
entrails	ooze
howlet	intestines
swelter	pot
venom	poison

2. Circle the meaning of each word as it is used in the poem.

swelter'd:	pale green	oozed out	smelly
charmed:	enchanted	golden	burned
fenny:	skinny	from the hills	from the marshes
fillet:	forked fangs	scaly skin	strip of meat

3. Read each phrase. If it includes alliteration, circle the letters that create the effect. If it doesn't include alliteration, cross it out.

> Like a hell-broth boil and bubble
>
> Days and nights has thirty-one
>
> Double, double, toil and trouble
>
> Fillet of a fenny snake
>
> Lizard's leg, and howlet's wing

4. Number the ingredients in the order they were added to the caldron.

_____ lizard's leg	_____ howlet's wing
_____ eye of newt	_____ tongue of dog
_____ blind-worm's sting	_____ toe of frog
_____ toad	_____ wool of bat
_____ fillet of a fenny snake	_____ adder's fork

Before You Read the Poem

Build Background

Tell students that the poem they are about to read is by Lewis Carroll, the same poet who wrote "You Are Old, Father William," which they read earlier in this unit. "Jabberwocky" is from Carroll's world-famous book, *Through the Looking-Glass*. Specifically, it appears in the chapter called "Humpty Dumpty." Students may refer to that chapter of the book if they would like to learn more about the Jabberwock. Otherwise, you may simply tell them that the Jabberwock is a kind of dragon. The poem tells the story of a deadly battle between the Jabberwock and a courageous young boy.

While You Read the Poem

This poem is fun to read aloud because of all the invented words in it. For the same reason, some of the words can be challenging to pronounce! Model how to pronounce invented words such as *gimble*, which probably starts with a hard /g/, but use your own judgment for these and any other made-up words. Only Lewis himself knew how the words were meant to be pronounced. Then form groups of students and have each group read one of the stanzas aloud.

After You Read the Poem

Elements of Poetry

Form: Rhyming Verse "Jabberwocky" is a poem in rhyming verse. Ask students to help you identify the rhyming pattern of stanzas 1, 2, 4, and 7, which is *abab*. Then direct their attention to stanzas 3, 5, and 6. The rhyming pattern in those stanzas is *abcb*. In the *c* line, Carroll makes up for the "missing rhyme" by creating rhymes within the line itself. In the third stanza, for example, the *c* line reads: "So rested he by the Tumtum tree." Since *he* rhymes with *tree*, we don't notice that the end of the *c* line doesn't rhyme with the end of the *a* line, a pattern established by the two previous stanzas.

Poet's Toolbox: Invented Words Virtually every other word in this poem has been invented by the author. You won't find these words in a dictionary, but you can guess what a lot of them might mean. Carroll has cleverly taken advantage of traditional settings, actions, and imagery to help suggest possible interpretations for this otherwise nonsensical poem. For example, we don't know what *brillig* means, but it probably has something to do with the weather, and other clues in the stanza suggest that the setting is probably dark and swampy. Talk about the other invented words with students. They will look at these words more closely on the second activity page.

Follow-up Activities

Students may work independently to complete the activities on pages 120 and 121.

Jabberwocky

1   'Twas brillig, and the slithy toves
    Did gyre and gimble in the wabe:
    All mimsy were the borogoves
    And the mome raths outgrabe.

2   "Beware the Jabberwock, my son!
    The jaws that bite, the claws that catch!
    Beware the Jubjub bird, and shun
    The frumious Bandersnatch!"

3   He took his vorpal sword in hand:
    Long time the manxome foe he sought—
    So rested he by the Tumtum tree,
    And stood awhile in thought.

4   And, as in uffish thought he stood,
    The Jabberwock, with eyes of flame,
    Came whiffling through the tulgey wood,
    And burbled as it came!

5   One, two! One, two! And through and through
    The vorpal blade went snicker-snack!
    He left it dead, and with its head
    He went galumphing back.

6   "And hast thou slain the Jabberwock?
    Come to my arms, my beamish boy!
    O frabjous day! Callooh! Callay!"
    He chortled in his joy.

7   'Twas brillig, and the slithy toves
    Did gyre and gimble in the wabe;
    All mimsy were the borogoves,
    And the mome raths outgrabe.

—Lewis Carroll

Understanding the Poem

Read each question and choose the best answer. You may wish to reread "Jabberwocky" as you work.

1. The Jabberwock appears to be _____ .
   - Ⓐ a wise old man
   - Ⓑ a horrible monster
   - Ⓒ a helpless little boy
   - Ⓓ a graceful, long-necked bird

2. The _____ probably has feathers and a beak.
   - Ⓐ Jubjub
   - Ⓑ Tumtum
   - Ⓒ Jabberwock
   - Ⓓ Bandersnatch

3. The deadly battle took place in front of the _____ .
   - Ⓐ slithy toves
   - Ⓑ borogoves
   - Ⓒ Tumtum tree
   - Ⓓ frumious Bandersnatch

4. "Callooh! Callay!" probably means something like _____ .
   - Ⓐ Achoo!
   - Ⓑ Pow! Bam!
   - Ⓒ Hip, hip, hooray!
   - Ⓓ You must be kidding!

5. This poem is probably based on stories about _____ .
   - Ⓐ Cinderella
   - Ⓑ knights and dragons
   - Ⓒ the Loch Ness monster
   - Ⓓ the search for hidden treasure

6. This use of made-up words suggests that the events in the poem _____ .
   - Ⓐ were real
   - Ⓑ were exciting
   - Ⓒ were also made up
   - Ⓓ could have actually happened

 Read and Understand Poetry • EMC 3326 • ©2005 by Evan-Moor Corp.

Name _____

Understanding the Poem

"Jabberwocky" has lots of made-up words. Still, you can almost guess what these words might mean. It helps to first decide whether the word is a noun, an adjective, or a verb. Here are some reminders:

- A **noun** names a person, place, or thing. Examples: *pond, forest, monster, knight*
- A **verb** is an action word. It tells what somebody or something does. Examples: *search, find, destroy*
- An **adjective** describes a noun. Examples: *dark* woods, *chilly* night

1. Decide whether each of these words is a noun, adjective, or verb. Write *n*, *a*, or *v* next to each word.

Bandersnatch _n_	gimble _v_	mome _n_	tulgey ____
borogove ____	Jabberwock ____	outgrabe ____	uffish ____
burbled ____	Jubjub ____	rath ____	vorpal ____
frabjous ____	manxome ____	slithy ____	wabe ____
galumphing ____	mimsy ____	toves ____	whiffling ____

2. Make up definitions for the following words. Follow the example.

Bandersnatch: <u>Noun. An animal that lives in the tulgey wood.</u>
<u>The Bandersnatch and Jubjub bird are mortal enemies.</u>

Burble: _____

Frabjous: _____

Gimble: _____

Jabberwock: _____

Mimsy: _____

Slithy: _____

Tove: _____

Whiffle: _____

Acrostic (uh-CROSS-tick)

In an *acrostic* poem, a word or short message is spelled out vertically using the first letter of each line. The hidden message in an acrostic is always related to the theme or main idea of the poem, as in this excerpt from a poem about Rosh Hashanah, the Jewish New Year.

Example:

R enewal
O f
S pirit
H ealing

from "New Year Prayer"
by Sarita Chávez Silverman

Alliteration (uh-lih-tuh-RAY-shun)

When several words that begin with the same sound are next to each other or close together, it is called *alliteration*. In this example, the words *bubble, bays,* and *babble* create alliteration. The *b* sound in the middle of *bubble, babble,* and *pebbles* also adds to the alliterative effect. Tennyson has used alliteration here to create water-like sounds to strengthen his images of the brook.

Example:

I bubble into eddying bays,
I babble on the pebbles.

from "The Brook"
by Alfred, Lord Tennyson

Ballad

A *ballad* is a song or poem that tells a story. Most ballads are written in *quatrains*, or four-lines stanzas, with patterns of rhyme that help make them easier to recite or sing by heart. Ballads are among the earliest forms of poetry, and were used long before printed texts to tell stories and remember events from history. Ballads are still written today. Some ballads continue to be passed along by word of mouth in what is called the *oral tradition*.

Example:

The selkie be a creature strange.
He rises from the sea to change
To human form, a weird one he,
When home it is in Skule Skerry.

from "The Great Selkie of Skule Skerry"
Traditional

Capitalization and Punctuation

The rules for using *capitalization* and *punctuation* marks are not always strictly followed in poetry. Some poets choose not to use capital letters or punctuation at all, as in the following example.

Example:

so much depends
upon

a red wheel
barrow

glazed with rain
water

beside the white
chickens

"The Red Wheelbarrow"
by William Carlos Williams

Read and Understand Poetry • EMC 3326 • ©2005 by Evan-Moor Corp.

Colloquial Language *(kuh-LOW-kwee-ul)*

Informal language and vocabulary that is part of everyday speech is referred to as *colloquial language*. Colloquial expressions include slang and familiar expressions. They are often used when a poet wants to reach simple, "regular" people or to show that they are speaking in a poem. By adding "you see" in these lines, the poet gives these words a colloquial, familiar tone.

Example:

His hands, you see, Mama says
were hard and callused.

*from "Her Daddy's Hands"
by Angela Johnson*

Contrast

When two things are compared, the writer points out differences between them. Often, noticing the *contrast*, or difference, between two things helps readers "see" what the poet is trying to show them. In this example, the poet contrasts a response to good and evil.

Example:

For the heart of a friend,
   open up the wall;
for poison and daggers,
   close up the wall;

*from "The Wall"
by Nicolás Guillén*

Couplet *(CUP-lit)*

When two lines in a poem rhyme, they are called a *couplet*. (Notice that the term includes the word *couple*, meaning "two.") This example has two couplets.

Example:

In Flanders Fields the poppies blow
   Between the crosses, row on row
That mark our place; and in the sky
   The larks, still bravely singing, fly

*from "In Flanders Fields"
by John McCrae*

Dactylic Foot *(dack-TILL-ick)*

Patterns of beats in a line of poetry are called *feet* (see "Foot," on the next page). A pattern that includes a stressed syllable followed by two unstressed syllables is called a *dactylic foot*. In this example, the stressed syllables are in boldface.

Example:

'**For**ward, the **Light** Brigade!
Charge for the **guns!**' he said:

*from "The Charge of the Light Brigade"
by Alfred, Lord Tennyson*

Dialog

When two or more characters have a conversation, it is called a *dialog*. Dialog can be included in poetry. When it is, some poets follow the same rules of punctuation used for writing dialog in prose (quotation marks, commas, and speaker words), as in this example. Some poets do not.

Example: "You are old, Father William," the young man said,
   "And your hair has become very white;
And yet you incessantly stand on your head—
   Do you think, at your age, it is right?"

*from "You Are Old, Father William"
by Lewis Carroll*

Elegy (ELL-uh-jee)

An *elegy* is a poem written for mourning or grieving. Usually, the poet mourns for the death of a person. In this example, the poet expresses sorrow over the destruction of a civilization and its way of life.

Example:

In the road lie broken arrows;
We have torn our hair in grief.
The roofs are gone from our houses;
Their walls are sullied and stained.
from "The Destruction of Tlatelolco"
Anonymous

Enjambement (on-joh-MAWE)

When a thought stops at the end of a line in a poem, we say the line has an *end stop*. When the thought continues from one line into the next, we call it *enjambement*. This term contains the French word for leg: *jambe*. That's probably why lines with enjambement are also called *run-on* lines. In this example, the first line has an end stop and the second has an enjambement.

Example:

I became the words I ate in you.
For better or worse
the apple doesn't fall far from the tree.
from "Seeds"
by Javaka Steptoe

Foot

When a poem follows a pattern of meter, each line may be divided into rhythmic units. Each of these rhythmic units is called a *foot*. Each foot is made up of stressed and unstressed syllables. In this example, the rhythmic unit is made up of an unstressed syllable followed by a stressed syllable (shown in boldface). There are two feet in each of these lines.

Example:

The **way** a **crow**
Shook **down** on **me**
from "Dust of Snow"
by Robert Frost

Free Verse

When a poem is written without a pattern of rhyme, meter, or line length, it is called *free verse*. Poets use words and images to help make free verse feel different from regular sentences, or *prose*.

Example:

First thing
outside my window
the wild world sings.
I wonder
how it would be
to fly over
my neighborhood,
from "Free as a ..."
by Linda Armstrong

Haiku (hi-KOO)

Haiku is a form of poetry that first began in Japan in the 1700s. A haiku always has three lines. In the "classic" form, the first and third lines have five syllables, and the second line has seven. A traditional haiku focuses on an image in nature. Even when haiku does not focus on nature, it usually presents a closeup look at a single detail.

Example:

Pushing through moist earth
tulips leave no room for doubt:
spring is here at last.
"Tulips"
by Sarita Chávez Silverman

Iambic Meter *(eye-AM-bick)*

When the rhythmic unit, or *foot* (see "Foot") in a poem is made up of an unstressed syllable followed by a stressed syllable, the poem has *iambic meter*. In this example, each line includes four iambic feet. This pattern is called *iambic tetrameter (teh-TRAM-ih-tur)*. The name includes the Greek term for *four: tetra*. In this example, the feet are separated and the stressed syllables are in boldface to help you see the pattern.

Example: We **are** / the **Dead**. / Short **days** / ago
We **lived**, / felt **dawn**, / saw **sun**/set **glow**,
from "In Flanders Fields" by John McCrae

Invented Words

Invented words are made up by the poet. You can usually guess what they mean by noting how they fit with the other words in the poem. What might *runcible* mean in this example?

Example: He has many friends, laymen and clerical,
Old Foss is the name of his cat;
His body is perfectly spherical,
He weareth a runcible hat.

from "How Pleasant to Know Mr. Lear" by Edward Lear

List Poem

In a *list poem*, the poet builds the poem by listing a series of things. Some list poems use patterns of rhyme or rhythm; others do not. This example has both.

Example:

Fillet of a fenny snake,
In the caldron boil and bake;
Eye of newt, and toe of frog,
Wool of bat, and tongue of dog,
Adder's fork, and blind-worm's sting,
Lizard's leg, and howlet's wing,—

*from "Round about the caldron go"
by William Shakespeare*

Lyric Poetry *(LIH-rick)*

Poetry that focuses on feelings and impressions is called *lyric poetry*. When they read a lyric poem, readers may think about similar feelings and experiences they have had, or they may imagine the feelings described by the poet. In this case, the poet shares his feelings about youth and old age.

Example:

Age, I do abhor thee;
Youth, I do adore thee.

*from "Youth, I Do Adore Thee!"
by William Shakespeare*

Metaphor *(MET-uh-for)*

A *metaphor* compares two things by presenting them as being almost identical. For example, a metaphor that compares snow to a white blanket would read: *The snow is a white blanket.* In this example, a farmer's backbone is compared to iron and earth.

Example:

His backbone is forged
of African iron
and red Georgia clay.

*from "The Farmer"
by Carole Boston Weatherford*

Meter *(MEE-tur)*

A regular pattern of rhythm is called *meter*. Writing made up of sentences that use meter is called *verse*. Writing made up of sentences that do <u>not</u> use meter is called *prose*. To feel the meter in this example, clap or tap for each syllable.

Example:

He reads, but he does not speak, Spanish,
He cannot abide ginger beer;
Ere the days of his pilgrimage vanish,
How pleasant to know Mr. Lear!

from "How Pleasant to Know Mr. Lear"
by Edward Lear

Narrative Verse

Narrative verse tells a story, or narrates. Narrative poetry does not always follow the rules of punctuation and capitalization used in prose stories. Narrative poems may also be told in rhyme.

Example:

one late afternoon
I came home from school feeling sorry
for an old woman living beneath the
elevated train below the station

from "My Grandmother Had One Good Coat"
by Tony Medina

Narrative Voice

The *narrative voice* in a poem belongs to the narrator, or speaker. Not all poems have a speaker, as in the example from "No!" In the second example, the narrator is someone speaking about her mother and grandfather.

Example:

No shade, no shine, no butterflies, no bees,
No fruits, no flowers, no leaves, no birds
    November!

from "No!" by Thomas Hood

Example:

His hands, you see, Mama says
were hard and callused.

from "Her Daddy's Hands" by Angela Johnson

Onomatopoeia *(aw-nuh-mah-tuh-PEE-uh)*

When a word sounds like the noise or sound that it stands for, it is called *onomatopoeia*. *Buzz* and *sizzle* are examples of onomatopoeia. In this example, the buzz of a bee is exaggerated to emphasize this onomatopoeia.

Example: Just then a bee flew close to their rail:—
"Buzzzzzzzzzz   zzzzzzzz   zzzzzzzz ZZZZZZZ."

from "Two Old Crows" by Vachel Lindsay

Parody *(PAIR-uh-dee)*

A *parody* is a work that copies the form (and sometimes the content) of an existing piece in order to make fun of it. The following examples show the beginning of a poem by Robert Southey which was later parodied by Lewis Carroll.

Example:

You are old, Father William, the young man cried,
    The few locks which are left you are grey;
You are hale, Father William, a hearty old man,
    Now tell me the reason I pray.

from "The Old Man's Complaints"
by Robert Southey

Example:

"You are old, Father William," the young man said,
    "And your hair has become very white;
And yet you incessantly stand on your head—
    Do you think, at your age, it is right?"

from "You Are Old, Father William"
by Lewis Carroll

Read and Understand Poetry • EMC 3326 • ©2005 by Evan-Moor Corp.

Personification *(per-sawn-uh-fuh-KAY-shun)*

When a writer describes something that is not human as having qualities or capabilities that are human, it is called *personification*. In this example, the poet describes trees as if they have the human capacity to make preparations, have wisdom, stand, and sleep.

Example:

Thus having prepared their buds
against a sure winter
the wise trees
stand sleeping in the cold.

from "Winter Trees"
by William Carlos Williams

Refrain *(ree-FRANE)*

A *refrain* is a group of lines that are repeated two or more times in a poem. When song lyrics include a refrain, it is called a *chorus*. In Tennyson's "The Brook," the following refrain is repeated at the end of four different stanzas.

Example:

For men may come and men may go,
    But I go on for ever.

from "The Brook"
by Alfred, Lord Tennyson

Repetition *(reh-peh-TIH-shun)*

When a poet uses the same word or words more than once in a line or in a poem, it is called *repetition*. Repetition can be used to emphasize a word or an idea in a poem. Repetition can also be used to create special sounds or rhythms in a poem. In this example, the repeating phrase "pile them high" echoes the opening words of the poem. It is used to emphasize the image of the number of men who die in wars.

Example: Pile the bodies high at Austerlitz and Waterloo.
Shovel them under and let me work—
    I am the grass; I cover all.

And pile them high at Gettysburg
And pile them high at Ypres and Verdun.

from "Grass" by Carl Sandburg

Rhyme Scheme

When two words end with the same sound, we say they rhyme. Poets use rhyming words to help make their writing sound different from prose. Rhyme can help words sound special or more musical. Rhyming words are usually placed at the end of a line in a poem. The pattern of rhyming words in a poem is called the *rhyme scheme*. In this example, the first and second lines rhyme and the third and fourth lines rhyme, so we can show this rhyme scheme as *aabb*.

Example:

And so, while Selkie kissed the lass,
She rubbed his neck with Orkney grass.
This had the magic power, you see,
To banish him from Skule Skerry.

from "The Great Selkie of Skule Skerry"
Traditional

Simile *(SIH-muh-lee)*

A *simile* compares one thing to another by using the word *like* or *as*. There are four similes in this example.

Example:

Youth like summer morn,
Age like winter weather;
Youth like summer brave,
Age like winter bare.

from "Youth, I Do Adore Thee!"
by William Shakespeare

Stanza (STAN-zuh)

A *stanza* is a group of lines in a poem. Usually, the lines in a stanza are related to each other in the same way the sentences of a paragraph "go together."

Example:

Wayfarer, your footprints are
the pathway and nothing else;   }1
wayfarer, there is no path,
the path is made as you walk.

As you walk the path is made
and when you gaze behind   }2
you see the path where
you'll never walk again.

from "Wayfarer, There Is No Path"
by Antonio Machado

Symbol (SIM-bull)

A *symbol* is person, a place, an object, or an action that stands for something besides itself. A flag, for example, can symbolize a state or country. In this example, the rose and the carnation are symbols of goodness and peace. The colonel's saber is a symbol of aggression and warfare.

Example:

"Knock, knock!"
"Who's there?"
"A rose and a carnation . . ."
"Open up the wall!"
"Knock, knock!"
"Who's there?"
"The colonel's saber . . ."
"Close up the wall!"

from "The Wall"
by Nicolás Guillén

Traditional Poetry

The authors of *traditional poetry* are unknown. Traditional poems have been recited and passed down from one generation to the next. Often, these poems were recited for years before anyone wrote them down. There are often several different versions of traditional poems. This traditional ballad is hundreds of years old.

Example:

A maiden from the Orkney Isles,
A target for his charm, his smiles,
Eager for love, no fool was she,
She knew the secret of Skule Skerry.

from "The Great Selkie of Skule Skerry"
Traditional

Translation (tranz-LAY-shun)

In a *translation*, words that were originally written in one language are expressed in another language. In this example, the words were first written in Nahuatl (*NAH-wahtel*), the language of the Aztecs.

Example:

Let us gather 'round and mourn
these events my friends,
mourn the end of the Aztec Nation.

from "The Destruction of Tlatelolco"
Anonymous

Davida Adedjouma

Davida Adedjouma began her writing career as an eight-year-old, writing poetry inspired by Gwendolyn Brooks and Nikki Giovanni. Her poetry and stories reflect the pride she has in her black American heritage. She also writes fiction and plays.

Linda Armstrong

Linda Armstrong started composing verses before she could write. She remembers sitting in the back seat of the family car inventing rhyming chants during family outings. She wrote poems on scraps of paper all through school, and she continued to write after graduating from college with a degree in English. Her first published poems appeared in *The National Anthology of High School Poetry,* and a collection of her poetry, *Early Tigers,* was published in 1995.

Basho

Basho is the pen name of Matsuo Munefusa, a Japanese poet who is considered the finest writer of haiku. He lived during the mid-17th century, when the haiku form was first developed. Basho expressed universal themes using the simple images of nature. His skillful focus on the natural world helped transform haiku from an unimportant pastime into a major form of Japanese poetry.

Michael Burgess

Michael Burgess is a writer and actor who was born and raised in South Carolina. "Lightning Jumpshot" is Mr. Burgess's first published poem for children.

Lewis Carroll

Lewis Carroll was the pen name of Charles Lutwidge Dodgson, who lived in England from 1832 to 1898, during the reign of Queen Victoria. He was an amateur magician and taught math by profession. Today, however, he is most famous as the author of *Alice's Adventures in Wonderland.* His poetry and stories are characterized by logic and puzzles. His themes are typically whimsical.

Robert Frost

Robert Frost was one of the major American poets of the 20th century. His poems are most often associated with New England life. His poetry nearly always was written in traditional verse forms, but the language of his poems shows a mastery of the rhythm and meter and the poetic use of the vocabulary and inflections of everyday speech.

Nicolás Guillén

Nicolás Guillén lived and wrote in Cuba. As a journalist of African Spanish descent, he wrote about the social problems faced by blacks in Cuba in the early 20th century. In addition to his own experiences, he was influenced by the American poet Langston Hughes, and like Hughes, his poetry reflects pride in his black heritage. Much of his poetry also reflects the political activism that dominated Cuban culture in the 20th century.

Thomas Hood

Thomas Hood was born in London in 1799. He was clever in the use of puns and was known as a humorist in his own lifetime, but his best-known poems today, "The Song of the Shirt" and "The Bridge of Sighs," express love and pity for suffering humanity.

Angela Johnson

Angela Johnson is the author of fiction and poetry for children. Her stories usually depict experiences common to children of all ages, but she is most noted for stories and poems that celebrate the uniqueness of African American families and highlight the value of close family ties.

Edward Lear

Edward Lear (1812–1888) lived in England during the reign of Queen Victoria. He was best known during his lifetime as an illustrator, focusing especially on scientific depiction of birds and other wildlife. Since his death, however, he has become known mainly for mastering the whimsical form known as the *limerick*, as well as for his other humorous poems. While the subject and form of his works vary, nearly all are characterized by an irreverent view of the world. Lear poked fun at everything, including himself.

Vachel Lindsay

Vachel Lindsay was born in Springfield, Illinois, in 1879. He was fascinated by common people, and his poetry reflects that interest. His poems were very rhythmic, and he performed them with chants, shouting, gesturing, and singing. He spent a number of years traveling across the United States, entertaining all who would listen to his works—often in exchange for food and shelter.

Antonio Machado

Antonio Machado was born in 1875 in southern Spain but moved to the capital, Madrid, as a child. When his father died unexpectedly, Machado and his brother Manuel helped support their family by writing and acting. They also traveled to Paris, where Antonio worked as a translator. By the time he finished his studies, Machado was already known as a poet. He held various teaching positions in Spain, but went into exile in France after the Spanish Civil War began in 1936. He died there in 1939, the year the war ended.

John McCrae

John McCrae (1872–1918) was born and raised in Canada. He served with Canadian forces as an artillery officer in the Boer War (1899–1902), fighting for the British Crown against the descendants of Dutch colonists in South Africa. McCrae later became a physician and served in that capacity in World War I. He tended the wounded during the Second Battle of Ypres in 1915, and wrote "In Flanders Fields" after helping to bury his friend Alexis Helmer after that battle. It is one of the most famous poems about that war in the English language.

Ian McMillan

Ian McMillan is an English author who has written a number of poetry books for both children and adults. He has been a poet, broadcaster, commentator, and producer for over 20 years. His poems have been published in numerous magazines, newspapers, and anthologies.

Tony Medina

Tony Medina grew up in the South Bronx of New York City. He is an English professor and has published several collections of poetry. He draws from his own experiences growing up in the projects of the city to create his art. The rhythm and language of his poems are filled with a wide range of emotions, and his poetry is easily accessible to young readers, as well as adults.

Carl Sandburg

Carl Sandburg was born to Swedish immigrant parents in Galesburg, Illinois, in 1878. His father worked as a blacksmith's helper for the railroad. Carl left school after eighth grade and worked for ten years before traveling for a year as a hobo. This experience made a lasting impression on him, and he developed deep admiration for American workers. Sandburg eventually finished college and began to work in journalism. With the publication of *Chicago Poems* in 1914, he began a long career as a poet, children's book author, and noted biographer of Abraham Lincoln. Sandburg has been recognized as one of the most distinguished American poets of the 20th century and was awarded the Pulitzer Prize for both poetry and biography.

William Shakespeare

William Shakespeare is generally considered the greatest playwright the world has ever known. He is equally famous for his sonnets, and is also recognized as the greatest poet in the English-speaking world. He lived and wrote in 17th century England. The subject matter of his poetry ranges across the breadth of the imagination. It is his mastery of the English language that sets him a level above all other poets.

Sarita Chávez Silverman

Sarita Chávez Silverman was awarded the Cowell Translation Prize in 1978 for her translation of poetry by Federico García Lorca. In 1996, one of her children's books was recognized as a commended title by the jury of the Americas Award for Children's Literature. Ms. Silverman works in curriculum development for young learners and in second-language instruction. Her creative interests reflect her mixed Jewish and Latino heritage.

Javaka Steptoe

Javaka Steptoe is an award-winning artist, designer, and illustrator. Both his parents were artists, and he credits them as being the major influences on his artwork. His art is characterized by the use of family as a recurring theme.

Alfred, Lord Tennyson

Alfred Tennyson (1809–1892) was a British poet laureate who was one of the most important English poets during the reign of Queen Victoria. He started writing poetry at the age of eight, and had almost completed a play written in blank verse by age fourteen. Queen Victoria gave Tennyson the title "Lord" in 1884.

Carole Boston Weatherford

Carole Boston Weatherford is a children's book writer who has written more than a dozen books. She looks to the past for family stories and fading traditions. She is noted for weaving poetry, history, chants, and percussion into school and community programs for people of all ages.

William Carlos Williams

William Carlos Williams (1883–1963) was born in Rutherford, New Jersey. His mother, who had a great influence on his work, was Puerto Rican and spoke Spanish. Williams worked as a physician, but he earned enduring fame as a poet. Dr. Williams was one of the great pioneers of modern free verse. The subject of his poetry often centers on the everyday circumstances of life and the lives of common people. In addition to poetry, he also wrote plays, novels, and biographies. His poems are often brief and written in free verse, and he employs lineation to great effect.

My Read & Understand

Poetry
Anthology

This book belongs to:

_____

THE SPECIAL SOUNDS OF POETRY

Line
Poems are usually made up of *lines.* Lines may be organized in stanzas.

I come from haunts of coot and hern,   *a*
I make a sudden sally   *b*
And sparkle out among the fern,   *a*
To bicker down a valley.   *b*

Rhyme Scheme
The pattern of rhyming lines in a poem is called the *rhyme scheme.* To show the rhyme scheme, use a different letter to label each line that ends with a new sound.

Stanza
A *stanza* is a group of lines in a poem. The lines go together like sentences in a paragraph. This stanza is one of 13 in this poem.

By **thirty** hills I **hurry** down,
Or slip between the ridges,
By twenty thorpes, a little town,
And half a hundred bridges.

Assonance
When the same vowel sound is repeated in words that are close together, it is called *assonance.* The sound of the vowels must be the same, but they need not be spelled the same.

Alliteration
When several words that begin with the same sound are close together, it is called *alliteration.* The beginning of the words must sound the same, but they need not be spelled the same.

Till last by **Philip's farm** I **flow**
To join the brimming river,
For **men may** come and **men may** go,
But I go on for ever.

Repetition
When a poet uses the same word or words more than once in a line or in a poem, it is called *repetition.*

Consonance
Consonance is the repetition of consonant sounds in words that are close together. Consonance may include the same beginning and ending consonants, as in *bubble* and *babble.* Or, it can use either beginning or ending consonants only, as with *pebbles, bubble,* and *babble.*

I **chatter** over stony ways,
In little sharps and trebles,
I **bubble** into eddying bays,
I **babble** on the **pebbles**.

Onomatopoeia
When a word sounds like the noise or sound that it stands for, it is called *onomatopoeia.* These words sound like flowing water.

from "The Brook" by Alfred, Lord Tennyson

Excerpt
An *excerpt* is part of a longer poem.

Poet
The name of the poet, or author of the poem, may go here or before the beginning of the poem. Sometimes, the author of a poem is unknown.

RHYTHM AND METER IN POETRY

Cannon to / **right** of them,

Cannon to / **left** of them,

Cannon in / **front** of them

Volley'd and / **thun**der'd;

Storm'd at with / **shot** and shell,

Boldly they / **rode** and well,

Into the / **jaws** of Death,

Into the / **mouth** of Hell

Rode the six / **hun**dred.

*from "The Charge of the Light Brigade"
by Alfred, Lord Tennyson*

Meter
A regular pattern of rhythm is called *meter*. The pattern is set by the arrangement of accented (stressed) and unaccented (unstressed) syllables.

Dactylic Foot
A pattern of poetic feet that includes one stressed syllable followed by two unstressed syllables is called a *dactylic foot*. The stressed syllables in this example are in boldface. Most lines have two dactylic feet. The feet in each line are separated by this symbol: /

Foot
When a poem follows a pattern of meter, each line may be divided into rhythmic units. Each of these rhythmic units is called a *foot*. A foot is made up of stressed and unstressed syllables. A line of poetry may include more than one foot.

Iambic Foot
An *iambic foot* has two syllables. The first one is unstressed and the second one is stressed. The iambic foot is one of the most common patterns of meter in poetry in English. Most of these lines have two iambic feet. A couple of the lines break the pattern with extra syllables.

Dust of Snow

The **way** / a **crow**

Shook **down** / on **me**

The **dust** / of **snow**

From a **hem** / lock **tree**

Has **giv**en / my **heart**

A **change** / of **mood**

And **saved** / some **part**

Of a **day** / I had **rued**.

—*Robert Frost*

Online Resources

The Academy of American Poets: http://www.poets.org

This comprehensive Web site includes over 1,400 poems, 500 poet biographies, and 100 audio clips of 20th- and 21st-century poets reading their own works (e.g., Gwendolyn Brooks, E. E. Cummings, Robert Frost, Langston Hughes, William Carlos Williams, and others). This site also includes the following:

- the Online Poetry Classroom, with free access to poetry curriculum units and other educational resources for teachers
- the National Poetry Almanac and Calendar, which track poetry-related events nationwide throughout the year
- information on National Poetry Month (April)

Lee & Low Books: http://www.leeandlow.com

Publishers of multicultural literature for children, Lee & Low Books has excellent poetry-related material on the Poetry Power page of their Web site. You'll find the following:

- ideas for bringing poetry into the classroom, by poet Pat Mora and literacy educator Regie Routman
- information on additional resources for incorporating poetry into primary classrooms
- digital movies of contemporary poets of color reading their works, including Tony Medina reading "My Grandmother Had One Good Coat" (included in *Read and Understand Poetry, Grades 5–6)* and Pat Mora reading "Song to Mothers" (included in *Read and Understand Poetry, Grades 2–3)*.

Audio Resources

In Their Own Voices—A Century of Recorded Poetry, ©1996, WEA/Atlantic/Rhino

This four-CD boxed set includes 122 poems recorded by their authors, including Robert Frost, Walt Whitman, William Carlos Williams (reading "The Red Wheelbarrow," included in *Read and Understand Poetry, Grades 5–6)*, and contemporary poets such as Maya Angelou, Lucille Clifton, Gary Snyder, Carmen Tafolla, and others. In compiling this impressive collection, poetry historian and recording producer Rebekah Presson drew from the Library of Congress archives, poets' personal archives, and recordings made on her 1980s radio show, *New Letters on the Air.* The collection also includes a printed booklet with additional information. Check your public library for a copy of this excellent collection.

The Writer's Almanac®

This is a short program (about five minutes in length) of poetry and history hosted by Garrison Keillor, heard daily on public radio stations. Check their Web site at http:writersalmanac. publicradio.org for local station listings. The Web site also has searchable archives.

Print Resources

Writing Poetry with Children by Jo Ellen Moore, ©1999 by Evan-Moor Corporation

Step-by-step lessons provide guidance for introducing a variety of poetic forms and supporting primary-age students in producing original poetry in each form.

Teaching 10 Fabulous Forms of Poetry by Paul Janeczko, ©2000 by Scholastic

Geared for intermediate grades (4–8), this volume introduces 10 poetic forms and supports students in planning and writing original poetry in each form.

See also the many fine poetry resource books listed on the Web sites noted above.

Artist to Artist

Page 8

1. D—worked for the post office
2. D—the poet's profession
3. C—paints for artists
4. C—thankfulness
5. B—the urge to create
6. A—David

Page 9

1. She says that her father gave her "his first name with an A at the end" and the poet's name is Davida Adedjouma.
2. She is grateful for the sacrifices he made, but she is sorry he never had a chance to make his own dreams come true.
3. Yes. At the end of the poem she asks what he is going to do now that he is retired.
4. Answers will vary. Examples could include:

bones	grew	day	teachers
tones	too	pay	preachers
phones	blue	say	bleachers
clones	drew	play	creatures

5. Answers will vary. Examples could include: construction crews, gardeners, maintenance workers, office workers.
6. Poems will vary.

Her Daddy's Hands

Page 12

1. D—a brick maker
2. A—Mama's daddy works all day.
3. D—toughened
4. C—city life in Alabama
5. B—loves him
6. D—loved his family and wanted to care for them

Page 13

1. Answers will vary. Example:

noisy	calloused	quietly	soft
quiet	soft	noisy	hard

2. "His hands, you see" and "those hands, you see"; "Down the red Alabama roads" and "along those red Alabama roads"

3.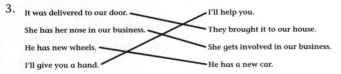

It was delivered to our door. —— They brought it to our house.

She has her nose in our business. —— She gets involved in our business.

He has new wheels. —— He has a new car.

I'll give you a hand. —— I'll help you.

4. He is quiet and gentle.
   He walks instead of drives the truck.
   He goes to church instead of to work.
   He wears his best black suit instead of work clothes.

My Grandmother Had One Good Coat

Page 16

1. A—in the city
2. C—the black wool coat
3. D—on tracks that go above city streets
4. B—riding commuter trains
5. C—generous
6. C—from his grandmother

Page 17

1. scowl—frown
   depressed—sad
   elevate—raise
   hesitate—pause
   taunt—mock

2. She was shouting insults at commuters, frowning and cursing because she was alone, cold, and hungry and had nowhere to live.
3. Yes. When the speaker comes home from school, the grandmother is there, and she goes to her closet to get the coat.
4. Answers will vary. Examples could include:

   Adds to: more immediate and sincere, allows interesting double meanings

   Takes away: hard to read and understand, hard to tell when someone is talking

5. They both care about the homeless woman.
6. They are both old.
7. She performs an act of kindness without making a show of it.

Seeds

Page 20

1. C—a parent
2. D—pictures
3. B—children grow up to be like their parents
4. B—apple recipes
5. A—words
6. B—They both draw pictures with words.

Page 21

1. "Like the trees, I grew/branches, leaves, flowers, and then the fruit.

2. "You drew pictures of life/with your words."

3. The apple doesn't fall far from the tree.—Children are like their parents.

   What's eating you?—What's bothering you?

   He ate his words.—He admitted his mistake.

   for better or worse—whether good or bad

   Mighty oaks from tiny acorns grow.—Children grow into adults.

4. Answers will vary. Example:

   The speaker probably learned some bad habits as well as good things from the parent.

5. a. enjambement
   b. end stop
   c. enjambement
   d. end stop
   e. enjambement
   f. end stop
   g. end stop
   h. enjambement
   i. end stop

The Farmer
Page 24

1. B—Georgia
2. D—the mule
3. C—a piece of land
4. A—cotton
5. D—strong
6. C—He has no spare time.

Page 25

1. plot: a storyline; a piece of land

   iron: to smooth out wrinkles; a type of metal

   stern: the back end of a ship; serious

2. He is in a southern field on a hot summer day with his mule.

3. Crossed out: c, d, g, h

4. That his African heritage and his American experience have made him as strong as tempered steel.

No!
Page 29

1. B—grass
2. A—noon
3. C—morning
4. D—November
5. B—gloomy
6. A—He thinks it's terrible.

Page 30

1. It is cloudy, so there is neither sunshine nor shade.

2. cheerful—full of cheer

   careful—full of care

   thoughtful—full of thought

   wasteful—full of waste

   artful—full of art

   fearful—full of fear

3. wastefulness—the quality of being wasteful

   thoughtfulness—the quality of being thoughtful

4. moon—noon

   steeple—people

   ease—bees

   member—November

5. moon—morn

   dawn—dusk

   shade—shine

   butterflies—bees

   fruits—flowers

Wayfarer, There Is No Path
Page 33

1. D—campfires
2. C—pathways blazed on the sea
3. A—to look
4. A—a blazing fire
5. C—Your life is guided by the choices you make.
6. D—each person must find his or her own way

Page 34

1. Circled: a, b, d

   Crossed out: c, e

2. No. You would sink into the water. OR There would be no marks left in the water for others to follow.

   He is not talking about actual paths or the actual ocean. He is talking about personal actions and time.

3. Noun: wanderer
   Meaning: a person who wanders

   Noun: teacher
   Meaning: a person who teaches

   Noun: believer
   Meaning: a person who believes

   Noun: listener
   Meaning: a person who listens

   Noun: traveler
   Meaning: a person who travels

   Noun: pretender
   Meaning: a person who pretends

Youth, I Do Adore Thee!

Page 37
1. C—bad teeth
2. C—a summer morn
3. D—pleasant things
4. B—youth and old age
5. B—Youth is best.
6. D—younger

Page 38
1. a. 5
   b. 3
   c. 6
   d. 8
   e. 2
   f. 7
   g. 4
   h. 1
2. tame—lame
   bold—cold
   care—bare
   sport—short
   Additional words will vary, but must rhyme.
3. M—Youth is nimble.
   S—Age like winter weather.
   S—Youth like summer brave.
   S—Age like winter bare.
   M—Youth is wild.
   M—Age is weak and cold.
4. grouchy—crabbed
   I think—methinks
   You—thee or thou
   do stay—stay'st
   morning—morn

New Year Prayer

Page 41
1. B—hopes and fears
2. A—humanity
3. D—a person's spirit
4. B—building a temple
5. C—hopeful and positive
6. A—all people should get along

Page 42
1. rewrite—write again
   reappear—appear again
   review—view again
2. More interpretations are possible without the punctuation.
3. harmony—a pleasing combination
   spirit—life force
   humanity—all human beings
4. healing, heart, harmony, humanity
5. Circled: all humans, human caring, compassion
6. Renewal Of Spirit, Healing Heart And Soul, Harmony Among Nations And Humanity

Winter Trees

Page 45
1. B—winter
2. D—complicated details
3. C—made ready
4. B—trees in early spring
5. D—remain dormant
6. A—early winter

Page 46
1. attiring—disattiring
   disattiring—getting undressed
   disagree—agree
   discomfort—comfort
   disbelieve—believe
   disadvantage—advantage
   discover—cover
   disharmony—harmony
   dishonor—honor
   dislike—like
2. Answers will vary. Examples: dismemorize, dislearn, disstudy, or others that follow the pattern.
3. They sleep standing up; they are outside in the cold; they are bare.

   Answers will vary. Examples could include: They let all the things they don't need fall away. They prepare for hard times before they come. They prepare for future growth.
4. Answers will vary.

Free as a...

Page 50
1. C—what it would be like to be a bird
2. C—birds' eggs
3. B—a window
4. B—a tree
5. A—free
6. A—bird

Page 51
1. outside my window—child

   a worm breakfast—bird

   tops of trees—bird

   I wonder—child

   streets like lines—bird
2. window wild world; tops of trees; between grass blades; one wild
3. a baby bird
4. the baby bird; this means doing something for the first time without a parent's help
5. Answers will vary.
6. Answers will vary.

Haiku Collection

Page 54
1. B—sunrise
2. C—be eaten by the worm
3. B—bloom in the spring
4. D—a father playing basketball
5. D—is loud and powerful
6. A—is the same as the number of syllables in the line

Page 55
1. a. *Hiker* sounds like *haiku*.

   b. Each line mentions the number of syllables that it has according to the haiku pattern: five, seven, five
2. thunders   lightning   storm
3. a. Tulips

Push/ing/through/moist/earth	5
tu/lips/leave/no/room/for/doubt:	7
spring/is/here/at/last.	5

   Lightning Jumpshot

Dad/dy's/voice/thun/ders	5
he/shoots/a/light/ning/jump/shot	7
through/a/sweat/y/storm	5

   Hiker

Walked/five/miles/to/day	5
and/sev/en/miles/yes/ter/day.	7
Five/more/to/mor/row.	5

Dust of Snow

Page 58
1. D—a hemlock
2. B—the crow
3. C—a light sprinkling of snowflakes
4. A—the life of a crow
5. C—was in the hemlock tree
6. A—better

Page 59
1. the speaker and the crow
2. No, because it doesn't snow everywhere. Setting does make a difference because the image of a crow, which is black, against a background of snow, which is white, is important to contrasting the "dark" and then the "light" mood of the narrator.
3. **light:** a dust of snow; snow on the ground; the speaker's mood after the snow fell

   dark: a hemlock tree; a crow; the speaker's mood before the snow fell
4. **crow:** snow

   me: tree

   heart: part

   rued: mood

   Additional words will vary, but must rhyme.
5. Answers will vary.

The Red Wheelbarrow

Page 62
1. A—cows
2. D—a wheelbarrow
3. C—coated
4. B—farm animals in the rain
5. C—shiny
6. C—a rain shower

Page 63
1. depends, upon, barrow, water, beside, chickens
2. wheelbarrow, rainwater
3. wheel + barrow = wheelbarrow

   rain + water = rainwater
4. sun—light

   chalk—board

   rail—road

   super—market

   under—water

   basket—ball
5. Answers will vary.

The Brook

Page 67
1. C—from its source to its end
2. A—a wilderness
3. D—sound it makes as it washes over rocks and stones
4. D—slows down in some places
5. B—will go on no matter what people do
6. D—imitate the sounds of flowing water

Page 68
Stanza 1: sudden sally

Stanza 2: hills, hurry; twenty thorpes; half, hundred

Stanza 3: Philip's farm, flow; men may

Stanza 4: bubble, bays, babble

Stanza 5: fret, field, fallow, fairy foreland; with willow-weed

Stanza 6: men may

Stanza 7: wind, with

Stanza 8: foamy flake; golden gravel

Stanza 9: men may

Stanza 10: steal, slide, sweet; hazel, happy

Stanza 11: slip, slide; gloom, glance; skimming swallows, sunbeam, sandy, shallows

Stanza 12: murmur, moon; linger, loiter

Stanza 13: men may

2. **Sounds:** bicker, chatter, bubble, babble, murmur

   Movement: sally, flow, slip, wind, steal, slide, move, linger, loiter, curve
3. Answers will vary.

The Charge of the Light Brigade

Page 73
1. C—saddles
2. A—the valley
3. B—a heroic cavalry charge in the Crimean War
4. C—attacking someone with a saber
5. B—honor the Light Brigade
6. D—could not win

Page 74
dismayed—dismay'd

wondered—wonder'd

blundered—blunder'd

through—thro

volleyed—volley'd

turned—turn'd

2. **brigade:** dismay'd, fade, made

   blundered: thunder'd, wonder'd, sunder'd, hundred

   reply: why, die

   bare: air, there

3. (Can) non to (right) of them
   (Can) non to (left) of them
   (Can) non in (front) of them

4. In stanza 3 they are riding in, and in stanza 5 they are retreating.
5. "Forward, the Light Brigade! Charge for the guns! Forward, the Light Brigade!"
6. He thinks they were very brave. OR He thinks they were heroes. Answers will vary.

In Flanders Fields

Page 77
1. B—blood
2. A—grave markers
3. D—honoring the dead by winning the war that took their lives
4. C—enemy
5. B—soldiers who died in a war
6. D—wants others to win the war

Page 78
1. It is still going on. The guns are still blasting and/or the speaker says to take up the torch.
2. We want you to finish the job we began.
3. **blow**—row, below, ago, glow, foe, throw, grow
   sky—fly, lie, high, die
4. In (Flan) ders (fields) the (pop) pies (blow)
   Be (tween) the (cross) es, (row) on (row)
   That (mark) our (place;) and (in) the (sky)
   The (larks) still (brave) ly singing, (fly)
   Scarce (heard) a(mid) the (guns) be(low.)

Read and Understand Poetry • EMC 3326 • ©2005 by Evan-Moor Corp.

Grass
Page 81
1. C—Bull Run
2. C—Waterloo
3. B—the grass that grows over battlefields
4. A—use a shovel to bury them
5. D—even the greatest battles are forgotten by the living
6. B—on a train

Page 82
1. the grass
2. Answers will vary.
3. Austerlitz, Waterloo, Gettysburg, Ypres, Verdun; all are associated with a famous battle.
4. Answers will vary.
5. The grass will cover the graves and erase signs of the battle.

The Wall
Page 86
1. C—the feast and the table
2. B—all of the hands
3. A—a weapon
4. C—a summer holiday at the beach
5. B—let the good in but keep out evil
6. D—a decision to choose good and reject evil

Page 87
1. scorpion—pain

   dove—peace

   saber—war

   mint—fragrance

   hummingbird—beauty
2. Answers will vary.
3. Open up the wall!
4. Knock, knock!, Who's there?, Close up the wall!
5. They are easy to remember. They have a strong rhythm. The lines can be predicted. If you don't hear part of the poem, it will be repeated.

The Founding of Mexico in 1325
Page 91
1. C—settled and began a great empire
2. D—prophecy, or vision of the future
3. A—Mexico
4. B—power
5. C—aggressive and warlike
6. B—honored parents and elders

Page 92
Answers will vary.

The Destruction of Tlatelolco
Page 95
1. B—grief
2. D—it is full of blood and abandoned weapons
3. A—war
4. D—weep and wail over the end of something
5. B—an Aztec god
6. C—writhing in the plazas

Page 96
1. Our hair is torn in grief.
   Our hands are beaten against the walls.
   We are protected by our shields in war.
   Dry twigs and wood are chewed for bread.
   Our mouths are filled with dirt and mud.
2. a. 6

   b. 3

   c. 5

   d. 1

   e. 4

   f. 2
3. Answers will vary.

The Great Selkie of Skule Skerry
Page 100
1. A—a seal
2. B—a strange creature
3. B—never
4. B—because he's not what he appears to be
5. C—A selkie can change forms.
6. C—used magic to outwit the selkie

Page 101
1. he is a weird one—a weird one he

   when he is a man—when he be man

   he has never kept a promise—But ne'er has he a promise kept.

   she was not foolish—no fool was she

   the selkie is a strange creature—The selkie be a creature strange.
2. strange—change

   he—be, Skerry, see, she

   accept—kept

   lass—grass

   isles—smiles

   bed—wed

   Additional words will vary, but should rhyme.
3. Answers will vary.
4. Answers will vary.

You Are Old, Father William
Page 104
1. D—his hearing
2. B—white hair
3. D—something you rub on your skin
4. A—a silly conversation between a father and son
5. D—Father William can balance a spoon on his nose.
6. C—humorous

Page 105
1. incessantly—e

   injure—g

   uncommonly—a

   locks—f

   supple—c

   couple—i

   suet—h

   clever—d

   suppose—b

2. said—head

   white—right

   son—none

   fat—that

   supple—couple

   locks—box

   before—door

   brain—again

   do it—suet

   law—jaw

   Additional words will vary, but should rhyme.
3. Answers may include any three: stands on his head; turned a back-somersault; ate a whole goose, including the bones and beak; balanced an eel on the end of his nose.

How Pleasant to Know Mr. Lear
Page 108
1. A—a ring
2. A—his nose
3. B—a room
4. C—Mr. Lear
5. D—Mr. Lear is imperfect, but fun to know.
6. A—has many friends

Page 109
1.
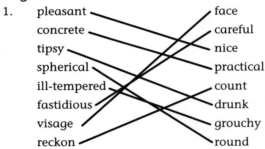
pleasant   face
concrete   careful
tipsy   nice
spherical   practical
ill-tempered count
fastidious drunk
visage   grouchy
reckon   round
2. Answers will vary.
3. enjambement
   end stop
   enjambement
   endstop

Two Old Crows
Page 112
1. D—a hunter
2. D—a fence rail
3. C—said
4. B—two crows and a bee
5. C—the bee caused the crows to fly away
6. C—He stuttered.

Page 113

1. Any four of the following:

   Two old crows sat on a fence rail.

   One crow asked the other crow a riddle.

   Why does a bee have a sword to his fiddle?

   B B B B B B B B B B B B B B B-cause OR

   Buzzzzzzzzzz zzzzz ZZZZZZZZ
2. cause and effect and nature's laws
3. its stinger
4. They sit around. They think more than they talk. They think about cause and effect. They mutter and stutter. They are afraid of bees.
5. Buzzzzzzzzzzzzzz zzzzzzzz zzzzzzzzzzzz ZZZZZZZZZZ
6. Answers will vary.

Round about the caldron go
Page 116
1. B—claw of cat
2. B—a toad
3. C—a snake's tongue
4. B—creating a powerful charm
5. A—a spell
6. D—entrails

Page 117
1. caldron—pot

   entrails—intestines

   howlet—baby owl

   swelter—ooze

   venom—poison
2. swelter'd: oozed out

   charmed: enchanted

   fenny: from the marshes

   fillet: strip of meat
3. Like a hell-broth boil and bubble

   Days and nights has thirty-one

   Double, double, toil and trouble

   Fillet of a fenny snake

   Lizard's leg, and howlet's wing

4. 1—toad

   2—fillet of a fenny snake

   3—eye of newt

   4—toe of frog

   5—wool of bat

   6—tongue of dog

   7—adder's fork

   8—blind-worm's sting

   9—lizard's leg

   10—howlet's wing

Jabberwocky
Page 120
1. B—a horrible monster
2. A—Jubjub
3. C—Tumtum tree
4. C—Hip, hip, hooray!
5. B—knights and dragons
6. C—were also made up

Page 121
Answers may vary. If not as shown here, ask students to replace nonsense words with familiar words to support their answers.

1. Bandersnatch n   mome n

   borogove n   outgrabe v

   burbled v   rath v

   frabjous a   slithy a

   galumphing v   toves n

   gimble v   tulgey a

   Jabberwock n   uffish a

   Jubjub n   vorpal a

   manxome a   wabe n

   mimsy a   whiffling v
2. Answers will vary.

Read and Understand Poetry • EMC 3326 • ©2005 by Evan-Moor Corp.